Clipper Programming by Example

Clipper Programming by Example

Paul Darling

Newtech
An imprint of Butterworth-Heinemann Ltd
Linacre House, Jordan Hill, Oxford OX2 8DP

A member of the Reed Elsevier plc group

OXFORD LONDON BOSTON
MUNICH NEW DELHI SINGAPORE SYDNEY
TOKYO TORONTO WELLINGTON

First published 1994

British Library Cataloguing in Publication Data
A catalogue record for this book is available from the British Library

ISBN 0 7506 2081 1

Typeset by Steve Heath
Printed and bound in Great Britain by Clays, St Ives plc

Contents

1 **Language overview** 1

Comment lines 2
The function average() 3
Variables and their declaration 3
Data Types 4
Say and get 6
Operators 7
Return 7
Summary 8
Problems 8

2 **Functions, procedures and operators** 9

Procedures 9
Functions 10
Return 10
Parameters 11
Declaring parameters 11
Using parameters 12
Pcount() 12
Arithmetic operators 13
Character operators 14
Right (), left (), substr () 14
Len () 15
At(), rat() 15
Upper(), lower() 16
Isupper(), islower() 16
Trim(), ltrim(), alltrim() 16
Array operators 17
Acopy(), aclone() 19
Len() 20
Ascan() 20
Asort() 21
Date operators 22
Day(), month(), year() 22
Dow(), cdow(), cmonth() 22

Dtoc(), dtos() 23
Empty() 23
Type conversion 24
Type(),valtype() 25
Summary 26
Problems 26

3 Console I/O 28

??/? 28
Devpos() 29
Row(), Col() 29
Clear 29
Cls 30
@ Clear 30
@ To 30
Dispbox() 31
Savescreen(), restscreen() 32
@ Say 32
@ Get 35
Read 37
@ Prompt, menu to 37
Setcolor() 39
Iscolor() 40
Set device to, set console, set printer 41
Transform() 41
Report form 42
Label form 43
Isprinter() 43
Memoedit() 43
Memoread(), memowrit() 46
Memoline(), mlcount() 47
Inkey(), Lastkey(), Nextkey() 48
Summary 48
Problems 49

4 Flow control 50

Do/function calls 50
Init/exit procedures 50

	Conditional expressions	52
	If	53
	If()	54
	Case	54
	For	56
	While	56
	Loop/exit	57
	Set key	57
	Summary	58
	Problems	58
5	**Files**	**60**
	Dbcreate()	60
	Select, dbselectarea()	61
	Use	62
	Close	62
	Dbusearea(), dbsetindex()	62
	Index on	63
	Descend()	64
	Set index	65
	Set unique	65
	Set order to	66
	Append blank/replace	67
	Field	67
	Delete, recall, pack, zap, reindex	68
	Seek, skip, go	69
	Set softseek	70
	Dbseek()	71
	Locate, continue	71
	Bof(), eof(), recno()	72
	Set filter	72
	Set relation	73
	Count, sum	73
	Copy to	74
	Append from	75
	Set printer to	75
	Fcreate()	76
	Fopen()	76

	Fwrite()	76
	Fread()	77
	Fseek()	77
	Fclose()	78
	Summary	78
	Problems	78
6	**Tables and code blocks**	**80**
	Achoice()	80
	User function	81
	Code blocks	82
	Aeval()	84
	Dbeval()	84
	Tbrowse	85
	GoTopBlock, GoBottomBlock	87
	SkipBlock	88
	RefreshCurrent(), refreshAll()	89
	Summary	90
	Problems	90
7	**Help, get and error systems**	**91**
	Help	91
	Set key 28 to help	91
	Get/Set functions	94
	The Get system	95
	GetNew()	95
	Readmodal()	97
	Reader	98
	Error handling	100
	Begin sequence	101
	Error class	101
	Errorblock()	102
	Errornew()	103
	Summary	104
	Problems	105

8 Further ideas 106

Pre-processor 106
Code blocks 108
Functions (and when to use them) 109
Macros 111
Set() 112
Summary 114
Problems 114

9 Solutions 115

Appendices

A Inkey codes 129

B Compiling, linking and making 132

C The CA-Clipper debugger 138

D The programmers editor, report and label writer and database utility 146

E Default file extensions 155

F Example program 157

Glossary 173

Index 177

1 Language overview

CA-Clipper started as a compiler for dBase, however over various releases the paths of dBase and CA-Clipper have diverged to such an extent that CA-Clipper can no longer be considered as merely a dBase compiler. There are many commands in CA-Clipper simply for compatibility with dBase, though as these are likely to disappear in the next full release of CA-Clipper they should not be used.

A program written in CA-Clipper, the source program, can be compiled and linked to produce an executable file to run under the MS-DOS operating system. A CA-Clipper source program is merely a series of commands held in one or more ASCII text file(s) which can be created using any editor or word processor capable of producing such files (if you do not have a suitable editor see Appendix C for a description of PE which is an editor provided with CA-Clipper). Each command is terminated by a carriage return which means that there should only be one command to a line, however if a command is too long for one line, lines can be 'joined' by placing a semi colon (;) at the end of each unfinished line.

The program below is presented as an example; don't worry if you do not fully understand it as each command will be discussed in detail later. The program held in a file called average.prg accepts three numbers and displays the average. It should be noted that as CA-Clipper is not case sensitive a mixture of both upper and lower case is often used to add clarity to a program as in the example below.

```
* Calculate Average
FUNCTION Average()
```

```
    LOCAL nFirst, nSecond, nThird, nAverage
    CLEAR SCREEN
    nFirst  := 0
    nSecond := 0
    nThird  := 0
    @ 0,0 SAY "Enter three numbers"
    @ 1,0 SAY "Number 1"
    @ 2,0 SAY "Number 2"
    @ 3,0 SAY "Number 3"
    @ 1,9 GET nFirst
    @ 2,9 GET nSecond
    @ 3,9 GET nThird
    READ
    nAverage := (nFirst + nSecond + nThird)/3
    @ 5,0  SAY "The average is"
    @ 5,15 SAY nAverage PICTURE "9,999.99"
RETURN nil
```

Comment lines

Comments are pieces of text placed in the source program. They are used to convey the purpose of a program or section of code to whoever is reading the program. Comments are ignored when the program is executed. There are various methods of inserting comments into a program. A common technique is to prefix a line with an asterisk whereupon the line is treated as a comment. Comments can also be placed on the end of any line simply by prefixing them with a double ampersand (&&) or a double forward slash (//).

All of the above methods only ‘comment’ one line at a time, if you wish to ‘comment’ more than one line of text you should use the C like method of starting with a slash-asterisk (/*) and finishing with an asterisk-slash (*/). There is also the command **NOTE** which ‘comments’ one line, however this command is for compatibility and therefore should not be used.

The function average()

This function is the start of the program and has the same name as the object file produced by the compiler. It is only required if the program is compiled with the /n option, as if this option is not used the function will be created for you by the compiler. There are however good reasons for the use of this option and we will cover some of them later.

Variables and their declaration

All variables in CA-Clipper must have their scope declared before they are used, you are not required to declare them yourself, however if you do you may only declare any one variable name once in any one procedure/function. Any variables not explicitly declared, will be declared as private by CA-Clipper at compile time. There are four scopes with which a variable can be declared, these are *Public, Private, Local,* and *Static.*

Any variable declared as **public** will be in scope throughout the program provided that another variable which is currently in scope has not been declared with the same name.

Private variables are in scope so long as the function or procedure in which they are declared is active, and provided another variable has not since been declared with the same name. That means that if FUNCTION A declares variable A and then calls FUNCTION B variable A will still be in scope. Private variables lose their value when the function in which they are declared is exited.

Local variables are similar to privates but with some important differences. These are that they are not in scope in any procedure/function called from that in which they are declared, and they cannot be used in any expression which is to be expanded using the macro command (&).

Static variables are slightly different due to the fact that they may be function wide or file wide. A function wide static is similar to a local with the exception that it's value is not lossed when the declaring function is exited. A file wide static is in scope while the code which is being executed is held in the same source code file as that in which the variable is declared, while the program is executing code held in other source files the variables value is retained.

Functions and Procedures may also be declared as static whereupon they can only be called from other functions and procedures held within the same source file.

Data Types

There are eight data types in CA-Clipper these are *numeric, character, logical, date, memo, array, block,* and *object.* A variable once declared can be assigned a value of any data type whereupon it takes on that type.

Numeric We have already met variables of this type in our program. A numeric variable can hold any number providing it has no more than 19 digits, it can have 18 decimal places and is always signed.

Character These variables can hold any of the 256 characters in the IBM character set. The size of a character variable is determined by the length of the string it contains and can be changed simply by changing this string. The maximum size of any one character variable is 64K.

Date As the name suggests these variables hold date values. The format for the date depends on the setting of Century and Date.

Logical These variables can only hold the values true or false. The CA-Clipper constants for these are .t. and .f. respectively.

Memo This is not actually a variable type but field type. It is required due to the fact that unlike character variables, character fields can not change their length. In memory memo fields are held in character variables, and hence are a maximum of 64K in size.

Array This is not a variable but a data structure. Each element of an array can be of any variable type including other arrays. The maximum number of elements in any one dimension is 4096. This does not prevent you from having 4096 elements each of which is another array, in this way the maximum number of elements is limited only by memory.

Block This type is new to CA-Clipper 5. Blocks or Code blocks as they are also known contain complied sections of code, we shall cover code blocks in detail later.

Objects CA-Clipper 5 introduced 4 pre-defined classes in a step towards OOP's. Each instance of a class is an OBJECT and is held in an object variable, we shall also cover classes later.

Say and get

Say is the command used to display formatted information at a precise point on the screen. The command:

```
@ 0,0 SAY "Enter three numbers"
```

displays the string 'Enter three numbers' on the screen starting at row 0 column 0.

Say also allows the formatting of the data using the **picture** extension so that if nAverage contained the value 1000.8 the command:

```
@ 0,0 SAY nAverage PICTURE "9,999.99"
```

will display the '1,000.80' however be warned if the picture is too short for the variable an overflow will occur and in the case of numerics all that will be displayed is a line of asterisks (strings are truncated).

Get is used to receive data from the user. As with say, get allows you to specify the coordinates at which to perform the get, and the format of the input using the picture command, it should be borne in mind that the length of a character string cannot be increased by the picture command and hence a variable initialised to 5 spaces will only allow the input of 5 or less characters even if used with a picture like 'XXXXXXX' (X is used for any character).

The get command also has the extensions **when** and **valid** to prevent the entry to and exit from the get respectively. The get command sets up which values are to be read and in which order. However, the get is not performed until the **READ** command is encountered.

Note

A character variable of length 0 (equal to "") will cause the input to be skipped, however any when or valid functions will still be processed.

Operators

Very few programs avoid the use of operators. These can range from simple assignment (:=) to complex mathematical operators such as modulus (%). They can also be used for the manipulation of character strings, creating relations between data files and comparison.

Return

A function or procedure finishes at the last command before the next function/procedure declaration or the end of the program file, whichever is first. When the return command is encountered program control is passed back to the calling routine. There may be any number of return commands in a function/procedure however, as excessive use can cause confusion it should be used sparingly and as a general rule few properly structured procedures need more than one return command. All functions must pass a value back to the calling routine this is done using the return command, the format of the command is:

```
RETURN <exp>
```

where <exp> is the data item to be passed back. If there is no value to be returned the function should return the value 'nil' as in the program above. As any data item can be returned it is possible to pass back an array and hence return more than one value.

Summary

In this chapter we have given you an overview of the CA-Clipper language. We have introduced functions and procedures, variables (both their scope and their types), comments, and how a program can communicate with a user. In the following chapters we will expand on all of these topics along with introducing files, methods of flow control and many of the other aspects which together make up the CA-Clipper language.

Problems

1.1 *Write a program which uses the* get *command to assign the variables* nHours *and* nMinutes *and displays the number of seconds since the start of the day.*

2 Functions, procedures and operators

In most languages, there are commands to enable logical sequences of statements to be grouped together. In some languages, these are GOTO and GOSUB while in others, they are SECTIONS and PARAGRAPHS In CA-Clipper, they are FUNCTIONS and PROCEDURES. This chapter shows how functions and procedures are defined and how they can be used. It also details what operators can be used on the different types of variables and shows that many of these operators are in fact functions.

Procedures

These are a left over from dBase but now with the introduction of functions and more recently the data value 'nil' they have little use. In CA-Clipper the only differences between procedures and functions are the ways in which they are called and the fact that functions return a value.

```
PROCEDURE Display(cName)
    @ 0,0 SAY cName
RETURN
```

If the above procedure were to be called with the command

```
DO Display WITH "Paul"
```

the name 'Paul' would be displayed at row 0 column 0. The command Procedure is the start of the definition and Return marks its end.

Functions

There are two types of functions — pre-defined and user-defined.

Pre-defined functions

These perform tasks such as displaying a box on the screen, supplying the date, converting a string to upper/lower case and detecting whether there is a printer connected. Functions held in libraries can also be considered pre-defined.

User-defined functions

As the name suggests these are functions defined by you as the user of the language.

```
FUNCTION Display(cName)
     @ 0,0 SAY cName
RETURN nil
```

If the above is called by

```
Display("Paul")
```

it will behave like the above procedure. As all user-defined procedures can be replaced with functions, we shall concentrate on functions from now on and only mention procedures where the differences are important.

Return

As was mentioned previously all functions must return a value even if that value is only 'nil'. It should be noted however that just because a function returns a value does not mean that the value has to be used.

Parameters

The final and most useful feature of functions is their ability to accept parameters. Parameters can be used to pass values to a function, and they can also be used to modify the behaviour of the function. Parameters are passed in one of two ways depending on whether it is a function or a procedure to which they are being passed. To pass the parameters *cName* and *cAddress* to the procedure Label you should list them separated by commas after the **with** keyword :-

```
DO Label WITH cName, cAddress
```

To pass the same parameters to the function Label you should list them again separated by commas but this time within parentheses.

```
Label(cName, cAddress)
```

If there are no parameters to be passed to a function you should still include the parentheses as opposed to procedures where you omit the **with** keyword along with any parameters.

Declaring parameters

There are two methods of declaration, these are to list the parameters within brackets after the function name as has already been shown or to list them after the key word **Parameter**. It makes no difference to the calling routine which way you declare the parameters as it is still called in the same manner however for the called function there is one major difference. Any parameters declared using the **parameter** key word are defined as private, any listed between parentheses are local, and hence the latter method is preferable.

Using parameters

Any value can be passed as a parameter to a function and, as it is becoming considered good programming style to only use local and static variables if a previously declared variable is to be used in a function, it must be passed as a parameter. When the function is entered the variables declared as parameters are created as privates/locals and a copy of the called parameters are then placed in the new variables. The only exception to this is if the variables are passed to the function by reference. There are two ways in which this can be done, these are to prefix the calling variable with an at sign :-

```
Label(@cName, @cAddress)
```

or simply use its name if the calling variable is an array or an object (the reason for this will be discussed later). If the contents of a variable which has been passed by reference are changed, the change will be made in the called variable, if the variable is only passed by value (as is usual) no changes will be reflected in the called variable.

Pcount()

When calling a function the calling routine has no way of knowing how many parameters (or even what types) can be passed. This can cause problems if the wrong number of parameters are passed, so CA-Clipper provides you with the function **pcount()** which when called returns the number of parameters that were passed to the current function. This means that if the desired number were not passed remedial action can be taken.

Arithmetic operators

The symbols *, /, %, +, -, **, and ^ are the arithmetic operators available in CA-Clipper. These symbols along with brackets () and the = & := assignment operators are used to perform arithmetic functions. In the program Average in chapter 1 there is the statement

```
nAverage := (nFirst + nSecond + nThird)/3
```

This adds the values nFirst, nSecond and nThird together, divides it by 3 and places the result in the variable nAverage. As CA-Clipper adheres to the order of precedence defined in mathematics (see the table below), if the brackets were omitted CA-Clipper would divide nThird by 3 and then add it to nFirst & nSecond. This is clearly wrong, hence the inclusion of the brackets.

Symbol	*Example*	*Priority*	*Description*
()	(a+b)/c	1	parenthesised operation
**	a**b	2	exponential
^	a^b	2	exponential
*	a*b	3	multiplication
/	a/b	3	division
%	a%b	3	modulus
+	a+b	4	addition
-	a-b	4	subtraction

Along with the above operators and any numeric variables, an arithmetic expression can contain any function which returns a numeric value. If a compound statement contains such a function then this function is evaluated before the rest of the statement. Besides any functions you write for inclusion in arithmetic expressions there are several pre-defined functions which can be of use such as **int()** which returns the integer part of a number and **max()** which returns the larger of two numbers.

Character operators

Of the arithmetic operators mentioned above the assignment and addition operators have use in character expressions. To concatenate two strings simply add them together

```
cName := "Paul " + "Darling"
```

will result in the string 'Paul Darling' being placed in the variable cName. As with arithmetic expressions, string expressions can contain functions.

Right (), left (), substr ()

Of all the pre-defined functions available those of most use are **right()**, **left()**, **substr()**, and **len()**.

Right() and **left()** accept two parameters. The first is the string on which the operation is to be performed, the second is the number of characters to be returned. When called these functions return the requested number of characters starting at one end or other of the string.

```
left(cName,4)
```

will return the string 'Paul' and

```
right(cName,7)
```

will return the string 'Darling'

Substr() behaves in a similar manner to the previous two in that it returns part of a string. It accepts three parameters which are the string, the starting position and the number of characters to be returned. If this last parameter is not passed it will default to the remaining number of characters in the string.

```
substr(cName, 6, 3)
```

would return the string 'Dar'

Len ()

Although this function does not return a string, it is often used with the above functions because, as the name suggests, it returns the length of the string passed.

```
len(cName)
```

would therefore return the number 12.

At(), rat()

At() returns the position of the first occurrence of a character within any given string. It requires the character to be sought and the string in which the character can be found, if however the character cannot be found at() will return 0.

```
at("a", cName)
```

will return the number 2. Rat() works in the same manner to at() however it starts searching from the end of the string and hence will return the position of the last occurrence of the chosen character so that

```
rat("a",cName)
```

will return the number 7. Rat() also returns 0 if the character could not be found.

Upper(), lower()

There is often a need for a string to be in a standard case, in order to do this CA-Clipper provides the functions **upper()** and **lower()** which convert the characters in a string to upper or lower case respectively.

```
cString := "Paul"
upper(cString)
lower(cString)
```

the above will assign "Paul" to the variable cString. It is then converted to upper case, having done this it is converted to lower case.

Isupper(), islower()

We have now shown how to convert a string into either upper or lower case, however we have no way of knowing the case of the original string and therefore if this operation is necessary. We can determine the case of a character by passing it to one of the functions **isupper()** or **islower()** which return true if the character is in upper case or lower case respectively. The problem with these functions is that they only report on the case of the first character in the string passed; to find the case of the whole string requires you to write a function which passes each character of the string to one of these functions. To complement these functions there are the functions **isalpha()** and **isdigit()** which return true if the character is alphabetic or numeric respectively.

Trim(), ltrim(), alltrim()

There are many occasions when a string will have leading or trailing spaces (sometimes both), these can be a nuisance especially when an exact comparison of two strings is required. The functions **ltrim()** and **trim()** (also called rtrim()) can be used to remove leading and trailing spaces respectively, they each take a character string as an input and return a string with the unwanted spaces removed. **Alltrim()** can be used to remove both leading and trailing spaces at the same time and is called in the same way.

```
alltrim("   Hello   ")
```

will return the string 'Hello'

Note

The original string is unaffected by the trim functions unless the output is used to overwrite the input.

Array operators

As has already been mentioned, each array element can be of any data type and so the operations that can be performed on an array element are the operations which are valid for any variable of that type. Having said that, there are also several operations that can be performed on an array itself. These are concerned with the creation and sizing of the array.

```
aArray1 := {}
aArray2 := {1,2,3}
```

will create a reference to an array called **aArray1** which contains no elements and a reference to an array called **aArray2** containing three numeric elements into which the values 1,2, and 3 are placed. To access the second element of array **aArray2** use

```
aArray2[2]
```

However, if the array has more than one dimension the commands:

```
aArray2[2][2] and aArray2[2,2]
```

will both access the same element. Once an array has been created elements can be added using the **aadd()** function. This function accepts two parameters, which are the array to which the element is to be added and the element.

```
aadd(aArray1, cName)
```

would add the value in the variable *cName* to the array **aArray1**.

```
ains(aArray1, 1)
```

would insert an element into array **aArray1** at position 1 and set its type to nil. When used, this function causes the last element in the array to be lost. To prevent this happening you should increase its size before performing the insertion; you can do this with the **asize()** function. This function accepts the array and the new size such that the command :

```
asize(aArray1, 5)
```

makes the array aArray1 have 5 elements irrelevant of how many elements it had before the command. The opposite of inserting an element into an array is deleting one, this can be done using the function **adel()** which also accepts the array to be affected and the position of the element but this time the element is deleted and all elements which came after it are moved up the array one position.

Like ains(), adel() does not affect the size of the array which means that after it is used there is an empty element at the end of the array. If you wish to place a value into each element of the array you could assign each element individually; however this is very time consuming and wasteful. An easier way is to use the function **afill()** which accepts the array as its first parameter and the value as its second. If only part of the array is to be filled this can be achieved by passing it a third (and, if necessary, a fourth) parameter. The third parameter afill() will accept is the position at which to start assigning the value, the fourth is the number of elements to be assigned.

```
afill(aArray2, 0, 2, 2)
```

will assign the value 0 to the second and third elements of the array aArray2.

Acopy(), aclone()

An array variable merely contains a reference to that array, and as such if it is used as a parameter then that array is passed by reference. It is because arrays are held in this way, that an array can not be copied simply by assigning it to another variable (this would merely create a second reference to the same array). To make a copy of an array in the summer 87 release of CA-Clipper you had to use the **acopy()** function, which requires the source and target arrays to be passed as parameters, these can be followed by the starting position and the number of elements to be copied, it is also possible to state the starting position in the target array. Since summer 87 could only use single-dimension arrays version 5's arrays present acopy() with a problem, and if used with a multi-dimension array, acopy() will only create a copy of the first dimension. To overcome this problem you should use the **aclone()** function which simply takes a source array as its only parameter and returns a reference to a complete copy of that array.

Len()

If you pass an array to the **len()** function it will return the number of elements in the first dimension of that array. As one function can be passed as a parameter to another function an array can be increased in length by one in preparation for insertion with the command :-

```
asize(aArray1, len(aArray1) + 1)
```

Once you have values stored in your array you may want to access the last element, this can always be found by using the **len()** function however this operation can also be accomplished by the use of the function **atail()** which accepts the array as a parameter and returns the value of the last element.

```
? aArray1[len(aArray1)]
? atail(aArray1)
```

will both display the same value (the last one in aArray1).

Ascan()

Ascan() is used to find an element within an array, it requires the array to be searched and the desired element as parameters, it can also accept the position number of the element within the array at which to start the search and the number of elements to be searched. If the element is found

ascan() will return its position otherwise it will return the number 0.

```
aArray := {"Tom", "Dick", "Harry"}
ascan(aArray, "Tom")
ascan(aArray, "John")
```

the first call will return the number 1, whereas the second will return a 0.

Asort()

We have so far seen how to build an array, how to add an element to the end, or how to insert it in the middle, how to delete it again and how to find it if its position is not known. The one other action which is often performed on an array is sorting. **Asort()** takes the array to be sorted as a parameter and returns a reference to the sorted array, it can also take two other parameters which are the start position and the number of elements if only part of the array is to be sorted.

```
aArray := {9,8,7,6,5}
aArray := asort(aArray)
```

After the above code is processed aArray will contain {5,6,7,8,9}.

Note

Although asort() returns a reference to a sorted array this is merely a reference to the original array. Therefore the above command could be replaced with

```
asort(aArray)
```

In this form asort() can only sort single dimensional arrays in an ascending order. If any other behaviour is required a code block must also be passed as a further parameter (see chapter 6).

Date operators

All data types use the assignment operators, however if you ignore assignment the only remaining data type for which operators have any meaning is Date. To create a date variable use the **ctod()** (character to date) function and pass it the date as a string, or the **date()** function which returns the system date as a date variable. The exact format of the date depends on the setting of century and date however for the purposes of this explanation we shall assume century is set to off and date to British.

```
ctod("01/08/92")
```

would return the 1st of August 1992 as a date. Once you have a date variable you can use + and – to add or subtract a number of days. You can also use – to subtract one date from another in which case the result is the number of days between the two dates.

Day(), month(), year()

A date variable can be split into its constituent parts by using the functions **day()**, **month()**, and **year()**. Each of these functions takes a date as an input and returns a number to indicate the day/month/year referred to by the date.

Dow(), cdow(), cmonth()

As well as knowing the day of the month it is often useful to know the day of the week, this can be found by using the function **dow()** which takes a date as an input parameter and returns a number starting with 1 for Sunday and finishing with 7 for Saturday. Associated with dow() is the function

cdow() which also takes a date as input but returns the name of the day as a string. In the same way as cdow() returns the day as a string **cmonth()** returns the name of the month.

```
cdow(ctod("01/08/92"))
cmonth(ctod("01/08/92"))
```

The first function will return the string 'Saturday' and the second 'August'.

Dtoc(), dtos()

While you can create date variables using ctod() it is sometimes useful to create a string representation of a date. This can be done using one of two functions depending on the format you require. **Dtoc()** is the exact inverse of ctod() so that

```
dtoc(ctod("01/08/92"))
```

will return the string '01/08/92', whereas dtos() returns the date in the format yyyymmdd.

```
dtos(ctod("01/08/92"))
```

will return the string '19920801'.

Empty()

This function is used to determine whether or not a variable is 'empty'. The phrase 'empty' is a little ambiguous due to the fact that this function can take an input parameter of any type. It will however always return the logical value 'true' if the input contains the contents as defined in the table overleaf for each data type. Please note that this function will return the logical value 'true' for a value that is logically 'false'.

Data Type	***Contents***
Array	Zero-length
Character	Spaces, tabs, CR/LF, or (“”)
Numeric	0
Date	CTOD(“”)
Logical	False

This means that

```
empty("          ")
empty(ctod("  /  /  "))
```

will both return .t., but

```
empty(2)
```

will return .f.

Type conversion

It is often necessary to convert a variable from one data type to another, in order to create date variables, to add a number to a character string etc.

In CA-Clipper providing the operation would make sense (i.e. you can't convert ‘Paul’ to a number) it is possible to convert any value of the types numeric, character, date and memo into another of these types and later you shall encounter functions to include logical in this list. To convert between types CA-Clipper uses a base type of character. That is to say that rather than provide a method of converting each type to each of the others it simply provides those to convert each to a character string and back again. We have already stated that memo fields are in reality character strings and so this one presents no problem. Likewise we have covered the use of **ctod()** and **dtoc()** to convert to and from dates.

This leaves us with numbers. To convert a string to a number use the **val()** function.

```
val("123")
```

will return the value 123 as a numeric and to convert back use the **str()** function. This function accepts three parameters of which only the first is required.

```
str(123.1, 5, 1)
```

will return the string `"123.1"`. That is a string containing the first value, 5 characters in length and with 1 decimal place. If the third parameter were to be omitted the number would be rounded to an integer and the string returned would be `"  123"`. If only the first parameter was passed the returned string would be 10 characters in length and contain the value `"     123.1"`

Type(),valtype()

Before a variable can be used its type must be known and while this may seem an obvious statement there are many occasions when this is not the case. One example of the programmer not being certain of the type of a variable is if that variable is an input parameter. When a function is called the calling routine is unaware of the type of parameters required or even the number of parameters and hence it is perfectly possible for a function to be called with an insufficient number of parameters each of which is of the wrong type. If a function is called in this manner there are two courses of action which it can take, one is to crash (not particularly friendly), the other is to detect the problem and take remedial action (either to correct the problem or report the error and exit). There are two commands which enable you to detect the type of a variable these are **type()** and **valtype()**. Both of these return the type of fields, expressions, public and private variables however, valtype() can also handle local and static variables and functions (both pre-defined and user-defined) and is therefore preferable. The functions take a single expression as an input and return an upper-case letter which denotes the type. The results are:

Value	***Meaning***
A	Array
B	Block
C	Character
D	Date
L	Logical
M	Memo
N	Numeric
O	Object
U	NIL

so that

```
valtype("Paul")
```

will return the letter C.

Summary

In this chapter you have seen how to define functions, how to pass values into them and how to return values from them. You have seen operators and learnt that functions can also be considered as operators. This chapter has covered many of the functions needed to perform operations on both character strings and arrays and has mentioned a need for code blocks which are covered in chapter 6.

Problems

2.1 Write a program which accepts two numbers and displays the larger.

2.2 Write a program which accepts a name, adds it to a 'welcome' message and displays it.

2.3 Write a program which takes the system date and displays it like '1, August 1993'.

3 Console I/O

There are many methods of reading from and writing to the screen, some of which can be used in conjunction with the set console, set device, and set printer commands to write to a printer. In this chapter we will show how to display information on the screen, how to get information from the user and how to print this information on the printer. We will also show you how to use colour and how to edit strings up to 64K in size.

??/?

The simplest method of displaying anything is to use the **??** and **?** commands. These display whatever comes after them at the current position. The difference between the two commands, although being slight is significant in that the **?** command prefixes the output with a carriage return and hence the first visible character displayed can be found at column 0 on the next line. Therefore

```
?? "Hello "
?? "World"
```

would display 'Hello World' where as

```
? "Hello "
? "World"
```

would be displayed on two lines. As with most CA-Clipper commands there are two functions which are equivalent to **??** and **?**, these are **qqout()** and **qout()** respectively. They are used as follows

```
qqout("Hello")
```

and

```
qout("Hello")
```

Devpos()

If you need to use one of the above commands but require control over the output it is probable that you need to move the cursor. This can be achieved using the **devpos()** function. Simply by passing it the desired coordinates this function will move the cursor to any point on the screen.

```
devpos(10,0)
?? "Hello"
```

will display the word 'Hello' at row 10 column 0. Note if we had used **?** it would have been displayed on line 11.

Row(), Col()

You now know how to move the cursor to any point on the screen; however before doing this you often want to know where the cursor is (perhaps so that you can return the cursor to this point later). This can be discovered by calling the functions **row()** and **col()** which return the current row and column positions respectively.

Clear

It is rare that a program which performs any kind of console I/O can avoid clearing the screen, and even if the whole screen is not cleared you will often find yourself clearing small areas of the screen. The first command to mention is **clear**. This command takes one of three parameters: *screen*, *memory*, and *all*. These clear the screen area, any memory variables which have been defined, or both (an example of which can be seen in the program in chapter 1).

Cls

You are probably familiar with this command already from MS-DOS, and as you would expect it simply clears the screen.

@ Clear

It is also possible to clear just a region of the screen by using the **@ clear** command. To specify the region to be cleared you should state the coordinates of the top left hand corner and the bottom right hand corner of the area to be cleared. If you omit the bottom right hand corner it will default to the bottom right corner of the screen.

```
@ 10,10 CLEAR TO 40,40
```

will clear the rectangle of screen between row 10, column 10 and row 40, column 40.

```
@ 10,20 CLEAR
```

will clear the screen from row 10, column 20 to the bottom corner of the screen.

@ To

Having cleared the screen there is often a wish to put a border around the area to be worked in. Of course you can do this by displaying the box characters in one of the ways we have already seen however a better method is to use the **@ to** command. As with **@ clear** this command accepts the coordinates of the box to be drawn

```
@ 10, 10 TO 20, 30
```

will draw a single line box between row 10, column 10 and row 20, column 30. If you wish to draw a double line box simply add the **double** key word after the second pair of coordinates. It is also possible to specify the colour in which the box is drawn by adding the colour string after the key word **color**, (for details on colour see later). If the **color** key word is omitted the box is drawn in the current colour.

```
@ 10, 10 TO 20, 40 DOUBLE COLOR "R/W"
```

will draw a double line box from row 10, column 10 to row 20, column 40 in red on white.

Dispbox()

An alternative method of drawing a box is to use the **dispbox()** function. The first four parameters are the coordinates of the box, the sixth is the colour string, however the fifth is what makes this function special.

This parameter specifies what type of box to draw, if it is omitted or passed any number other than 2, a single line box will be displayed. If a 2 is passed the box will be drawn with double lines. If you want a different type of box you can state which characters to use, to do this pass an eight or nine character string. The first eight characters are for the edge, starting at the top left corner and cycling around. The ninth is used to fill the box. If instead of a string a single character is passed it will be used to draw the border. In this way you can draw a box and blank out the middle in one function call.

```
dispbox(10, 10, 20, 40, "╓─╖║╜─╙║ ")
```

will draw a box from row 10, column 10 to row 20, column 40. This box has double lines at the sides and single lines top and bottom.

Savescreen(), restscreen()

We have now seen how to clear a small area of the screen. This can be used for popup boxes etc., but you will probably find that you need to re-display the area of screen under the box when finished. There are two steps in this process, the first is to save the area of the screen which is about to change. The **savescreen()** function is passed the coordinates to be saved, and returns a character string containing the screen data. Having finished with the screen it can be restored using the **restscreen()** function. This function accepts five parameters, the coordinates at which to perform the restore followed by the string returned from **savescreen()**.

```
/* Savescreen demo.  Save as demo.prg */

FUNCTION Demo

    LOCAL cScreen
    cScreen := savescreen(5, 5, 7, 19)
    dispbox(5, 5, 7, 19)
    @ 6,6 SAY "Press any key"
    inkey(0)
    restscreen(5, 5, 7, 19, cScreen)
RETURN nil
```

You should find that the above program displays a single line box on the screen containing a message, once you pressed a key it should have re-displayed whatever was on the screen before the program was run.

@ Say

You have now seen how to position the cursor and then display data as two separate steps however it is possible to combine these steps as well as to add formatting and colour using the @ **say** command. The simplest form of this command is

```
@ 10,5 SAY "Hello"
```

this will display the word 'Hello' at row 10, column 5. The colour of the output can be specified by adding the **color** key word followed by the required colour string.

```
@ 10,5 SAY "Hello" COLOR "R/W"
```

this time it will be displayed in red lettering on a white background. The formatting is done with the picture clause. After the **picture** key word should be a character string or function which returns a character string or, a function containing the formatting information. This information can take the form of a character by character template, a translation function, or both separated by a space. If both a function and a template is to be used the function must come before the template. Translation functions are identified by preceding the single charcter name by an at sign '@'.

Function	***Description***
B	Left-justify numbers.
C	Display CR after positive numbers.
D	Display dates in the format specified by set date.
E	Display dates and numbers in British format.
R	Non-template characters to be inserted.
X	Display DB after negative numbers
Z	Display zeros as blanks.
(	Surround negative numbers with brackets.
)	Surround negative numbers with brackets, suppress spaces.
!	Convert alphabetic characters to upper case.

Template character	***Description***
A	Only alphabetic characters.
N	Only alpha-numeric characters.
X	Any character.
9	Only numbers (and sign for numerics).
#	Digits, signs and spaces.
L	Display logicals as ‘T’ and ‘F’.
Y	Display logicals as ‘Y’ and ‘N’.
!	Convert alphabetic characters to upper case.
$	Display a dollar sign before number.
*	Display an asterisk before number.
.	Specify decimal point position.
,	Specify comma position.

To use a translation function the first character in the string must be an @ followed by the single character name of the function.The functions and template characters are shown in the preceeding two tables.

If the variables below are initialised and used as follow:

```
nPositive := 2462.4
nNegative := -345.01
nTel  := 0815894499
cName := "Paul Darling"

@ 0,0 SAY nPositive PICTURE "9,999.99"
@ 1,0 SAY nPositive PICTURE "@c"
@ 2,0 SAY nNegative PICTURE "@x"
@ 3,0 SAY nNegative PICTURE "@("
@ 4,0 SAY nTel      PICTURE "@r 999-999-9999"
@ 5,0 SAY cName     PICTURE "@!"
```

they will display

```
2,462.40
     2462.4 CR
      345.01 DB
(     345.01)
 81-589-4499
PAUL DARLING
```

@ Get

As this is the main method of data input in CA-Clipper it may come as a surprise to find that since CA-Clipper 5 was released @ **get** is no-longer a command. When compiled this command is converted into calls to the get object class, however you do not need to use the get system to use the get command. Like @ **say**, the @ **get** command requires the coordinates at which to work

```
@ 10,5 GET data
```

will perform a get for the variable `data` at row 10, column 5. The variable `data` must be *character, date, numeric* or *logical* in type. The **picture** and **color** key words can be used in the same way as with @ say. In addition to the previously stated picture functions get can use the following:-

Function	***Description***
K	Delete default text if first key is not a cursor key
S<n>	Allows horizontal scrolling within character gets. <n> is an integer that specifies the width of the region.

Although the picture clause means that the get command is quite flexible, its power can be greatly enhanced by the addition of the **when** and **valid** key words.

When/valid should be followed by expressions or functions which return a value of true if the get is to be entered/left respectively and false if not. One further feature of the get command which can be very useful is the ability to add a prompt to the get. This is done by inserting a say command prior to the get, this say can have its own picture and color clauses. As was mentioned in chapter 1 the get command merely details which variables are to be got and in which order, they are not actioned until the **read** command is encountered. If this is done the message is displayed at the coordinates provided and the get performed immediately following the message.

```
FUNCTION GetTest

/* Example of get input */

  CLS
  cName := "               "
  cFadd1 := "               "
  cFadd2 := "               "
  cFadd3 := "               "
  cFpost := "      "
  lSecond := .f.
  cSadd1 := "               "
  cSadd2 := "               "
  cSadd3 := "               "
  cSpost := "      "

  @ 0,0 SAY "Name     " GET cName PICTURE "@!" ;
            VALID (left(cName,1) != " ")
  @ 1,0 SAY "Address " GET cFadd1
  @ 2,9 GET cFadd2
  @ 3,9 GET cFadd3
  @ 4,0 SAY "Post code " GET cFpost VALID !empty(cFpost)
  @ 5,0 SAY "Second address " GET lSecond PICTURE "Y"
  @ 6,0 SAY "Address " GET cSadd1 WHEN lSecond
  @ 7,9 GET cSadd2 WHEN lSecond
  @ 8,9 GET cSadd3 WHEN lSecond
  @ 9,0 SAY "Post code " GET cSpost ;
            VALID !empty(cSpost) WHEN lSecond
  READ
RETURN nil
```

When you have run the above program you will find that you are prompted for a name and two addresses. You are also asked if the second address is to be used. You should find that you are unable to leave the name field until there is a character in the first position and that all the characters are converted to upper case. Once you enter the post code field you will find that you are unable to leave until you have entered a value (this time it can be at any position). You should also find that you can only enter the second address if you have stated that it is to be used.

Read

As has already been mentioned the read command is used to activate the currently defined gets, however a brief description of the get system can greatly increase the use of this command. When each get command is encountered a get object is placed at the end of an array called *getlist* (CA-Clipper defines this array as public). This array is then processed by the read command which on completion clears it ready for the next series of gets. To prevent getlist being cleared read can accept the keyword **save** so that the gets can be re-activated later. An unpleasant side effect of the fact that getlist is a public variable is that if a when or valid function contains a read command it will re-activate the previous gets, this can be prevented by declaring a local array in the function.

Note

To nest gets a local array called getlist should be declared in the lower level functions.

@ Prompt, menu to

Most systems have some form of menu; in early systems these were just simple lists from which the desired option was selected. However these days the majority of menus are either a bounce bar or ring menus. Both of these types of menus can be implemented by the **@ prompt** and **menu to** commands. The menu options are first placed on the screen using the @ prompt command, its use is similar to @ say in that you state the row and column at which to display the option along with the text however there is an optional fourth parameter which is preceded by the keyword **message**, and is the additional text to be displayed when the option is highlighted. This text is displayed at column 0 on the row specified by the set message command. When all the prompts have been displayed the menu can be activated with the menu to command, this command requires a numeric variable into which the number of the selected option is placed (or 0 if escape is pressed). If this variable already contains a value the menu will start with that option highlighted, the highlighted option is displayed in the current enhanced colour the rest are displayed in the standard colour (for more on colour see later).

```
LOCAL nOption
CLS
SET MESSAGE TO 24
@ 5, 5 PROMPT "New"   MESSAGE "Start a new document"
@ 6, 5 PROMPT "Open"  MESSAGE "Open an existing document"
@ 7, 5 PROMPT "Close" MESSAGE "Close this document"
@ 8, 5 PROMPT "Save"  MESSAGE "Save changes"
nOption := 2
MENU TO nOption
```

will display a bounce bar menu containing four options which when started will have the second option highlighted. As each option is highlighted the appropriate message will be displayed on row 24. To make this a ring menu simply change the coordinates such that all the prompts are on the same line.

Note

If you want the messages to appear on different lines or in different colours replace the message text with a code block which displays the text (see chapter 6 for code blocks).

Setcolor()

Many of the commands we have seen so far have allowed the inclusion of a colour string, this string is a character string containing between 1 and 5 colour codes. These codes are for *standard*, *enhanced*, *border*, *background*, and *unselected*.

Standard	is used for all standard screen output.
Enhanced	is used for selected gets and highlights.
Border	is used to colour the edge of the screen (not EGA or VGA).
Background	is not used.
Unselected	is used for the colour of unselected gets.

Each of these codes consists of 2 colour codes separated by a forward slash (the first is the foreground colour and the second is for the background). Each of these colours can be made **bright** by adding a plus sign and can be made to **blink** by adding an asterisk to the letter. The letters can be replaced with numbers, however a mixture of letters and numbers is not allowed. If numbers are used adding 7 to the foreground colour will cause the colour to be bright, and adding it to the background will cause the foreground colour to flash. The colours are listed in the table overleaf (only the first 8 are background colours).

Colour	*Code*	*Number*
Black, Space	N	0
Blue	B	1
Green	G	2
Cyan	BG	3
Red	R	4
Magenta	RB	5
Brown	GR	6
White	W	7
Gray	N+	8
Yellow	GR+	14

For commands and functions which do not have a colour option it is possible to use the **setcolor()** function to alter the current colour combination. If called with no parameter this function will return the currently selected colours, however by passing a colour string to this function and assigning the return value to a variable it is possible to change the current colours and to be able to change them back at a later time.

Iscolor()

We have now shown you how to add colour to your applications, however you may want to run the same program on two or more computers in which case it is possible that you may not have a colour monitor. When CA-Clipper displays colour on a monochrome monitor it uses grey scales which, with some colour combinations are very difficult to distinguish, it would therefore be preferable for your program to be able to detect the type of output and select its colours appropriately. This can be done with the help of the **iscolor()** function which returns true if the computer has a colour graphics card installed.

Set device to, set console, set printer

We have seen how to send information to the screen however these commands simply send information to the current output device and so, if we want to send anything to the printer all we have to do is change the output device, this can be done with the **set device to** command or the **set printer** command. Set device takes one of the two keywords **screen** and **printer** and is required if you wish to print using @ say, however if you only wish to use console commands such as ? and qout() (i.e. those which do not require a row and column) set printer is sufficient. If the new output device is the printer, the output will be echoed to the screen unless the console is set to off.

```
SET CONSOLE OFF
SET PRINTER ON
? "This will be sent to the printer"
SET PRINTER OFF
SET CONSOLE ON
```

this will direct all output to the printer, write the line of text and then return to using the screen.

Note

If you use @say to print information, using a row number which is less than the last one used will cause a form feed to occur as in

```
SET DEVICE TO PRINTER
@ 1, 0 SAY "This is the first line"
@ 0, 0 SAY "This line will cause a form feed"
SET DEVICE TO SCREEN
```

Transform()

We have now seen how to send information to the printer, we have also seen that information can be formatted using picture clauses however this can not be used if you wish to use ? to print. This problem can be overcome with the use of the **transform()** function which takes the value to be formatted and the picture string to be used and returns a string containing the formatted output.

```
? transform(123456.3, "999,999,999.99")
```

will display the string "123,456.30" on the current output device.

Report form

We have now seen how to produce reports, however writing reports is a time consuming business and so to speed up this process simple tabular reports can be produced with a **report form** command. This command takes the name of the report definition file (as a string variable or a literal enclosed within parentheses) created using RL (see appendix D) and applies it to the current file. The output can be sent to the printer by adding the key words **to printer** to the command. If the report should be sent to a file the key words **to file** followed by the filename (again held in string variable or as a literal enclosed within parentheses) should be added. The output will be copied to the screen unless the keyword **noconsole** is also added to the command. If a number is added to the command then only that many records starting from the current position in the file are used in the report, the report can further be restricted by the addition of **while** and **for** clauses.

```
USE customer
REPORT FORM (customer) TO PRINTER ;
                       FOR left(cpost, 2) == "BS"
```

will print the report held in the customer definition file for all records in the customer file which have a postcode starting with the letters BS, it will also echo the report to the screen. If this definition file is changed (by adding columns etc.) the report produced will change but the command used remains the same.

Label form

We have now seen how report definition files produced by RL can be used to print reports, however RL can also define label definition files. These files can then be used by the **label form** command to print labels. This command uses many of the keywords associated with report form (all of the ones shown above) but can also use the keyword **sample** which will print labels containing asterisks and then ask whether you require more samples so that the alignment can be checked.

Isprinter()

It is all very well sending information to the printer but this is a useless (if not dangerous) thing to do if there is no printer connected. To prevent this a call should be made to the function **isprinter()** which will return true if the printer is connected and ready to print.

Memoedit()

We have already stated that memo fields are in reality simply character variables and that character variables can have their values assigned/altered using @ **get**, however as character variables can be up to 64K in size it would be nice to be able to modify such variables using a text processor, memoedit() enables you to do this. Memoedit() can accept 13 parameters, but as all of them have default values and none are compulsory the best way to call it is

```
memoedit()
```

This will use the whole screen for data entry and, if the function is exited by pressing control-w will return whatever was typed in. If you wish to edit an existing character string then this string should be passed as the first parameter. The next four parameters specify the coordinates of the window in which the editing is to take place. After the coordinates come four parameters which define how the edit is to behave, the first being a logical which states whether editing is to be allowed (as opposed to simply displaying the string), the next is the name of a user function (see later) this is followed by the length of the data lines, which if not equal to the width of the window will cause either the full width of the window not to be used or the window panning across the text depending on which is the wider. After the line length comes the tab size which defaults to 4 spaces but can be changed. Once these have been passed you can specify the row and column in the string at which the cursor is to be positioned on entry to the function and following these the starting row and column positions within the window.

Note

The text row counts from 1 whereas the other three row and column parameters count from 0.

```
memoedit(cText,5,5,20,40,.t.,"KeyPress",35,4,3,5,0,1)
```

This will allow the text held in the variable cText to be edited in the window 5.5 to 20.40. the line length is 35 characters. and any tab characters are replaced by 4 spaces. When called the cursor is placed on the 6th character of the 3rd line of the text and is positioned on the 2nd character of the 1st line in the window.

If a user function is specified, it is called when memoedit is first called, when an unknown key is pressed, and when there are no more keys to process. The function is passed three numeric parameters, these are the *edit mode*, and the *row* and *column* the cursor is at in the text. The modes are 0 no keys to process, 1 and 2 an unknown key has been pressed, and 3 memoedit() is being initialised. After having taken whatever action is required, the user function must return a numeric code to tell memoedit() how to proceed. These codes are detailed below.

Code	***Action***
0	Perform default action
1-31	Process requested action corresponding to key value (such as F1).
32	Ignore unknown key
33	Treat unknown key as data
34	Toggle word-wrap mode
35	Toggle scroll mode
100	Perform word-right operation
101	Perform bottom-right operation

When a key is pressed which is not recognised by the memoedit function a call is made to the user-defined function `KeyPress`. Below is a list of keys recognised by memoedit()

Key	***Description***
Up arrow	Move up one line
Down arrow	Move down one line
Left arrow	Move left one character
Right arrow	Move right one character
Ctrl-Left arrow	Move left one word

Key	Description
Ctrl-Right arrow	Move right one word
Home	Move to the beginning of the current line
End	Move to the end of the current line
Ctrl-Home	Move to the beginning of current window
Ctrl-End	Move to end of current window
PgUp	Move up one page
PgDn	Move down one page
Ctrl-PgUp	Move to beginning of text
Ctrl-PgDn	Move to end of text
Return	Go to beginning of next line
Delete	Delete character at cursor
Backspace	Delete character to left of cursor
Tab	Insert tab character
Insert	Toggle insert mode
Ctrl-Y	Delete current line
Ctrl-T	Delete the word to the right
Ctrl-B	Reform paragraph
Ctrl-W	Exit function returning new text
Esc	Exit function returning old text

Memoread(), memowrit()

While memo variables can be stored in memo fields this is not the only way to store them. Any text file (which is no greater than 64K in size) can be read into a memo variable and then edited using the memoedit() function. **Memoread()** is the function used to read in a text file, it takes the name of the file to be read as an input parameter and returns the contents as a string. **Memowrit()** can be used to write a text file, it takes the filename and the string which is to be written as parameters and returns a logical value to indicate whether the function was successful. If the filename does not contain a pathname these functions will look for the file in the current DOS directory and in the case of memowrit() if the file already exists it will be replaced.

```
aString := memoread("c:\autoexec.bat")
aString := memoedit(aString)
memowrit("c:\autoexec.bat", aString)
```

will put the contents of the autoexec file into the variable aString, allow this string to be edited and then rewrite the file.

Memoline(), mlcount()

As memo variables are in fact merely character variables, if you require one or two lines from within the memo you could technically use substr() however this could prove difficult if word wrap is used. A better method of extracting a line is to use the **memoline()** function. This function takes a memo variable, the number of characters per line, the number of the desired line, the number of spaces used for each tab and a logical to specify whether word wrap is on or off as parameters. Only the first parameter is required and if called in this way it will return the first line (to a maximum of 79 characters). If word wrap is on memoline() will format the text for the stated line length and each line can be returned. If on the other hand word wrap is off and memoline() is called with a line length which is shorter than that used to create it only the requested number of characters will be returned from the start of each line. Associated with this function is **mlcount()** which returns the number of lines in a memo variable, it accepts the same parameters as memoline() with the exception of the line number.

```
nLine := mlcount(cText, 20, 4, .t.)
? memoline(cText, 20, nLine, 4, .t.)
```

will display the last line in the memo variable cText, which is formatted with a line length of 20 characters, a tab size of 4 characters and word wrap set to on.

Inkey(), Lastkey(), Nextkey()

The last method of input we shall look at is the **inkey()** function. This function accepts a single parameter indicating the number of seconds to wait for a key to be pressed. If this parameter is omitted the function will not wait, whereas if the parameter passed is zero the function will only return when a key has been pressed. **Inkey()** returns zero if no key was pressed otherwise it will return the ASCII value of the key pressed. (For a list of the key values see Appendix A.) To convert this value into the character use the **chr()** function. This function takes a number and returns a character. The inverse of **chr()** is **asc()** which takes a character and returns its ASCII value. When a key is pressed it is placed into the keyboard buffer, **inkey()** reads the next key in this buffer however before it is read its value can be found by calling the **nextkey()** function. Once this key has been read (using inkey() or any other method to read the keyboard), the value of the last key which was read can be found by calling the **lastkey()** function.

Summary

In this chapter you have seen how to write to the screen and the printer both directly and through the use of definition files, how to get input from the users, and the functions associated with these actions. You have also seen how to change the colours, how to format the output and how to read, write, and edit large amounts of text.

Problems

3.1 *Write a function which displays a box and returns the screen which has been over-written. The function should accept the box characters and the coordinates.*

3.2 *Write a function which performs a get on a 20 character string in a 10 character window.*

3.3 *Write a program which calls* memoedit *within a window. You should include a user function which displays the cursor position.*

4 Flow control

So far we have seen how to construct simple programs, we have also seen how commands can be grouped together to form functions. However all the programs we have seen behave in the same manner, that is to say they start at the beginning and continue until they reach the end. While programs of this type have their uses, no program of any size can completely avoid the use of flow control. In this chapter we will cover the various flow control structures which are available in CA-Clipper, we will also cover conditional expressions which are an integral part of these structures. All of the control structures covered in this chapter can be nested to any level providing that for each opening statement there is the appropriate closing statement.

Do/function calls

We have already covered functions and procedures however it should be noted that a function call is a branch and as such is a form of flow control.

Init/exit procedures

There are two special types of procedures which can be defined in CA-Clipper, these are the init procedures and the exit procedures. These procedures can contain any code which can be placed in any other procedures or functions however it is the fact that they can only be called by the system (and not by your own programs) that make them special. These procedures are usually used for housekeeping tasks such as ensuring that all files are closed and the screen is cleared before leaving the system.

There is always one init procedure defined by CA-Clipper which defines how the system should handle errors and perform other housekeeping functions, this procedure is called CLIPINIT and is always called first, however you can define any number of others. Apart from CLIPINIT the order in which init procedures are called is not defined with the one exception that any procedures defined in the same file as the start-up procedure/function will be called last (for more about multi file programs see Appendix B).

The other type is the exit procedure which as its name suggests is called before the program is left. Again there can be any number of these procedures in a program and the only ordering which takes place is that those procedures which are defined in the start-up file are called first.

```
STATIC cScreen

INIT PROCEDURE Start
    cScreen := SAVESCREEN(0, 0, maxrow(), maxcol())
RETURN

EXIT PROCEDURE End
    RESTSCREEN(0, 0, maxrow(), maxcol(), cScreen)
RETURN
```

if the above were included in a program, on leaving the program would restore what was previously displayed.

Note

Although any init procedures that are defined in the start-up file are called last if there are more than one procedure of this type their order is not defined. This is also true of exit procedures.

Conditional expressions

At the heart of all flow control is a condition, conditions are expressions which return a logical value. An expression must contain two values of the same type separated by a relational operator, (the exception is a logical variable or a function which returns a logical value, which can be used as an expression by itself), all relational operators have equal precedence and therefore are evaluated from left to right.

Operator	***Description***
<>, !=, #	Not equal
$	Substring (characters only)
<	Less than
<=	Less than or equal to
>	Greater than
>=	Greater than or equal to
=	Equal to
==	Exactly equal to

Two or more expressions can be joined using logical operators. All logical operators have an equal precedence which is lower than the one assigned to relational operators. The logical operators are **.not.** (or **!**), **.and.**, & **.or.** When more than one expression is joined CA-Clipper will evaluate the minimum necessary to provide the answer so that if

```
nVar1 := 10
nVar2 := 20
```

in

```
nVar1 == 10 .AND. nVar2 == 20
```

both conditions will be evaluated as both must be true (and the first one is) whereas in

```
nVar1 == 10 .OR.  nVar2 == 20
```

only the first will be evaluated as only one must be true but in

```
nVar1 == 12 .OR. nVar2 == 20
```

again both will be evaluated as the first is false (the expression will still return true though due to the second).

If

This is the first flow control command that we shall consider. It allows blocks of code to be executed/skipped depending on the value of an expression. If the result of the expression is true all commands following up to the next **endif** will be executed, if there are commands to be executed when the expression is false you can either use a second **if** command or you can use the **else** keyword. When **else** is used it is possible to specify two blocks of code, one to be executed for each outcome of the expression (true and false). If the command is nested the **else** will apply to the last incomplete **if** command

```
? "the number is "
IF nNumber > 10
   ?? "greater than 10"
ELSE
   IF nNumber == 10
      ?? "equal to 10"
   ELSE
      ?? "less than 10"
   ENDIF
ENDIF
```

the above will display whether the number is greater than, equal to, or less than 10 depending on it's value.

If()

As well as the **if** command CA-Clipper has an **if()** function. This function accepts three parameters, the first is a condition, the second the value to be returned if the condition is true, and the third the value to be returned if the condition is false

```
IF nNumber == 10
   ? "True"
ELSE
   ? "False"
ENDIF
```

could therefore be written as

```
? if(nNumber == 10, "True", "False")
```

the return value can also be assigned to a variable and the second and third parameters can be function calls (but not procedure calls as they must return a value).

Case

Rather than writing a nested if structure, where the conditions are very similar CA-Clipper provides the **case** command such that

```
IF nOption == 1
   Func1()
ELSE
   IF nOption == 2
      Func2()
   ELSE
      IF nOption == 3
         Func3()
      ELSE
         Default()
      ENDIF
   ENDIF
ENDIF
```

can be written as

```
DO CASE
CASE nOption == 1
   Func1()
CASE nOption == 2
   Func2()
CASE nOption == 3
   Func3()
OTHERWISE
   Default()
ENDCASE
```

when a case statement is encountered the program will jump to the first condition which is true, processing will then proceed until the next **case** condition, the **otherwise** keyword, or the **endcase** keyword is met whereupon the program will jump to the next command after the endcase statement. If there is no condition which evaluates to true, and the **otherwise** keyword has been included then this code will be executed. If it is not included the program will simply jump to the command following the **endcase** statement and continue. Unlike many other languages CA-Clipper will allow any combination of conditions in a case statement so that the following is valid

```
nOption := nMenu()  && user defined menu function
DO CASE
CASE cUserLevel == "ordinary"
   Default()
CASE nOption == 1
   View()
CASE nOption == 2 .AND. lEdit
   Edit()
ENDCASE
```

in the above if cUserLevel is equal to 'ordinary' the function **Default()** will be called irrelevant of which option was selected, if not the next expression is evaluated. If option 1 was selected then the **View()** function is called; however if option 2 was selected the value of the logical variable lEdit is checked and only if it is true will **Edit()** be called.

For

We have now seen how to state whether or not to execute a block of code the last two control structures involve repeating blocks of code. The first of the repeat structures we shall look at is the **for/next** statement. If you know how many times you wish a block of code to be repeated it can be enclosed in a **for/next** loop. The **for** command requires a numeric variable to act as a counter, the starting and finishing values, and the value by which the counter should be incremented/decremented prefixed by the keyword **step** (if the counter is to be incremented by one the keyword **step** and the value **1** can be omitted).

```
FOR nCounter := 1 TO 20 STEP 2
   ? nCounter
   UserFunc(nCounter)
NEXT
```

the above will display all the odd numbers between 0 and 20 and call the function `UserFunc()` passing each value as a parameter.

While

If you do not know how many times a block of code should be executed it can be surrounded with the **do while/enddo** loop structure. This will continue to loop as long as the condition remains true.

```
nOption := nMenu()
DO WHILE nOption > 0
   DO CASE
   CASE nOption == 1
      nOption1()
   CASE nOption == 2
      nOption2()
   ENDCASE
   nOption := nMenu()
ENDDO
```

The above loop will continuously call the function **nMenu()** until it returns a value which is less than 1. If menu returns a value of 1 or 2 it will call the functions **nOption1()** or **nOption2()** respectively.

Loop/exit

For both *for/next* and *do while/enddo* you can specify either **loop** or **exit** (or both). **Loop** when encountered causes the program to jump to the top of the currently executed loop where it re-evaluates the condition/increments the counter. **Exit** will cause the program to jump to the command after the next *next/enddo* statement.

Set key

All the structures we have covered so far have been procedural in that the thread of processing can be followed through the code without it being run, however there is a way to make the program be event driven by the use of the **set key** command. This command allows the user to execute procedures in any order simply by pressing an associated key whenever the program is in a wait state. The most obvious example of when this is of use, is to use the F1 key to call for help, which as it can not be predicted as to when help will be needed it can not be coded in the normal way. The command requires two parameters the first being the inkey() code of the key to be assigned (see appendix A) and the second is the name of the procedure to be called.

```
SET KEY 28 TO Help
```

will call the procedure Help when the F1 key is pressed (28 is the inkey() code for F1). When called this procedure is passed three parameters, the first is the name of the calling procedure, the second the number of the line being executed when the key was pressed, and the third the name of the variable which was being read when the key was pressed. The maximum number of keys which can be defined at any one time is 32 one of which is taken by CA-Clipper pre-defining the F1 key to help, however when a key definition is no longer required it can be removed by setting a key without a procedure name.

```
SET KEY 28 TO
```

will remove the definition.

Note

Any procedures called in this way should have a neutral effect on the state of the system in that the current file, the current colour, etc. should not change on exit.

Summary

In this chapter you have seen that expressions are the corner-stone of flow control. We have covered both the IF statement and the IF() function, we have also seen the CASE statement and both the DO WHILE and FOR NEXT loops. We ended the chapter with an introduction to the SET KEY command.

Problems

4.1 *Write a function which accepts a character and a number and returns a string which contains number copies of character.*

4.2 *Write a program which accepts any number of exam marks (input to be terminated by any entry of -1), puts them into the following bands and then reports on the results.*

A:100-85 B:84-70 C:69-55 D:54-40 E:39-30 U:29-0

Your input routing should validate the input to prevent the entry of numbers greater than 100.

4.3 *The Fibonacci number sequence starts with the numbers 1 and 1, each subsequent number is the sum of the previous two numbers. Write a program which displays the first twenty.*

4.4 *Write a menu function which takes four arrays (for row, column, option, and message) and an initial option number as parameters and returns the number of the selected option.*

5 Files

In this chapter we shall look at the ways in which CA-Clipper can access DBF and TEXT files. Although the release of CA-Clipper 5 has meant that these are only two of many different types of files that can be accessed, they are still the most important. With DBF files most of the commands used now have equivalent functions (most of which start with DB), and where it is appropriate we shall look at these functions. The structure of a DBF file is very simple. Each file is divided into records, you can have as many records in a file as will fit on your disk. Each record is divided into fields, there is a maximum of 1024 fields allowed in any one record, and each field can be any of the following types *character*, *numeric*, *date*, *logical*, or *memo*. You have already encountered many TEXT files in the form of the source code you have written, and you have probably seen many other examples. The structure of a text file is quite simple in that it merely contains lines of text usually terminated by a carriage return followed by a linefeed. The uses of text files are too numerous to mention; however examples are print files and data transfer (both of which will be covered in this chapter).

Dbcreate()

Before anything can be done with a file it has to be created, this is done with the **dbcreate()** function. This function accepts two parameters, the first is the name to be given to the file, the second is a 2 dimensional array containing the structure of the new file. Each field in the file corresponds to an element in the first dimension of the structure array, and its properties are detailed in the second dimension. This second dimension has four elements, two character strings for the field name (maximum of 10 characters) and field type (this can be abbreviated to the first letter of the type) and two numerics detailing the field length and the number of decimal places. All elements must exist, the default number of decimal places is always zero, and the lengths for memos and dates are 10 and 8 respectively. If the file is to contain fields of type memo a second file will be created with the extension DBT in which the data is held.

```
aStruc := {}
aadd(aStruc,{"cName","c",30,0})
aadd(aStruc,{"cAdd1","c",50,0})
aadd(aStruc,{"cAdd2","c",50,0})
aadd(aStruc,{"cPost","c",8,0})
aadd(aStruc,{"cTel","c",15,0})
aadd(aStruc,{"nInvoice","n",10,0})
DBCreate("customer",aStruc)
```

The above will create a data file called customer.dbf in which customers names and addresses can be stored.

Select, dbselectarea()

CA-Clipper uses workareas to separate files from one another, if a file is opened in an area previously used by another file then the other file along with any indexes is first closed. Each workarea has a number and an associated alias (see later), either of which can be used to identify it, CA-Clipper supports 250 workareas. The functional equivalent of **select** is **dbselectarea()**, this function accepts the alias/number as a parameter. If workarea 4 has the alias customer

```
SELECT 4
SELECT customer
DBSelectArea("customer")
```

are all valid commands that will cause area 4 to become the current workarea.

Use

Use opens an existing data file (along with its memo file if available) and any indexes as specified. It can also be used to assign an alias if required, if you do not assign an alias it will default to the filename. If the keyword **new** is added **use** will open the file in the next available workarea, thereby ensuring that you do not inadvertently close one file by opening another.

```
USE customer INDEX name, invoice NEW
```

will select the next available workarea, assign to it the alias customer, open the data file customer along with its indexes name and invoice, and cause name to be the currently active index.

Close

If you issue the command **use** without specifying a file the data file in the current workarea will be closed. This can also be done with the **close** command which has the added advantage of being able to close all files which are currently open by adding the keyword **all**.

```
close all
```

will therefore close all the open data files in all the workareas.

Dbusearea(), dbsetindex()

Dbusearea() is the function which can be used to open files and as all of the necessary options are passed as parameters to it, it is of most use when the name of the file to be opened is held in a variable. The main problem in using this function to replace **use** is that it can not open any indexes, to do this you must use the **dbsetindex()** function

```
DBUseArea(.t.,,"customer")
DBSetIndex("name")
DBSetIndex("invoice")
```

will open the customer file in the same way as the previous **use** command. When dbsetindex() is first called it opens the desired index and causes it to be active, each subsequent call opens an additional index but has no effect on the previously open and active indexes.

Index on

When a record is added to a file it is always added to the end of that file and if subsequently its key value were to be changed this would not affect its position in that file. This is rarely of much use as not only do you need to be able to store data but you need to be able to retrieve it in an ordered manner; this can be accomplished using indexes. Indexes work in much the same way as an index on a book in that they hold references to the data file. You may have up to 15 indexes open for a file at any one time. To create an index file use the **index on** command. This command requires the key expression and the filename of the new index separated by the keyword **to**. The expression can be of any length up to a maximum of 250 characters however the longer the key the larger and more inefficient the index will be, there is also a rule that keys within an index should all be of the same length. The index key can be as simple as a single field name or as complex as the return value of a function. It is even possible to index a file based on a field in a related file (for more on relations see later) although many programmers shy away from this. Keys can be of the types *character*, *numeric*, *date*, and *logical*, however if a key is to be compiled from fields of more than one type (as is often the case), each part of the key should be converted to character. If we use the previous file

```
INDEX ON cName TO name
INDEX ON cPost TO post
INDEX ON nInvoice TO invoice
INDEX ON cPost + str(nInvoice, 15) TO complex
```

will create four indexes called name.ntx, post.ntx, invoice.ntx, and complex.ntx, the first two are simple character indexes, the third a simple numeric index, and the fourth an index based on the composite value of the post code and the invoice number. As the action of creating an index closes all previously open indexes in the current workarea complex will be the only active index.

Descend()

All indexes are created in ascending order, if you need an index in descending order (for dates for instance) the key should be converted to its complement value. This can be done using the **descend()** function which takes a value of the types character, logical or numeric and returns its complement in the same type, however if it is passed a date it will return a value of type numeric.

```
INDEX ON descend(cName) TO name
```

will create an index on the field name in reverse alphabetic order. It should be noted that if the field cName contained the value 'Paul' this value will not be held in the index, but rather its complemented value. To find this record in the index you would have to look for the result of `descend("Paul")`

Set index

We have now seen how to create indexes on an open file, but as creating an index closed all previously open indexes and as, while an index is open any additions or changes to the file are reflected in that index (the exception being with unique indexes) means that it is not necessary to create it every time it is opened, we need a method of opening more than one index for the currently open file. This is done using the **set index** command. This command closes all currently open indexes and then opens any indexes which are listed after the **to** keyword.

```
SET INDEX TO name, invoice
```

will perform the same function as the calls to **dbsetindex()** mentioned earlier.

Note

As dbsetindex() does not close any previous indexes to completely replace set index with this function you should first call to dbclearindex() which closes all open indexes in the current workarea.

Set unique

When an index is created it is possible to state whether duplicate keys should be included in the index. Note this does not prevent the record being saved, merely its existence being reflected in the index. This can be done in one of two ways either by **set unique on** or by adding the keyword **unique** to the end of the **index** command. It should also be noted that as records which have been marked for deletion are included in the index but not shown that if the entry in the unique index is for a deleted record, no records for that key will be visible while that is the current index, to correct this the file should be packed (see later).

Set order to

We have seen how to open indexes and have stated that when more than one index is open the active index is the first one opened. We have also stated that you can have up to 15 indexes open for any one file and, that while an index is open all changes to the file will be reflected in it. With all of the above being true it makes sense to keep all relevant indexes open at all times however this presents us with a problem, it would be very inconvenient if we had to close and then re-open all the indexes merely to cause a different one to be active. Fortunately this is not the case, the active index can be changed using the **set order to** command. **Set order to** accepts the number of the index which is to be active, this number is derived from the order in which they are opened so that

```
SET INDEX TO name, invoice
```

will cause name to be index 1 and invoice to be index 2. It is also possible to

```
SET ORDER TO 0
```

This will cause all the indexes to remain open but for the file to be in record number order. Note when the active index is first opened the record pointer is placed at the top of this index, however if the active index is changed using **set order to** the record pointer remains on the same record irrelevant of its position in the new index.

Append blank/replace

Now we have seen how to create and open files we need to be able to add records, this is a two stage process. First a blank record must be added to the end of the file this is done with the command **append blank**. Once a blank record has been added to the file the data has to be saved in that record. There are two ways to do this, the first is to use the alias (->) and assignment (:=) operators

```
customer->cName := "Paul"
```

will cause the field cName in the file whose alias is customer to be assigned the value 'Paul'. If customer is the file in the current workarea the alias can be replaced with the keyword **field** so that the above command could be replaced with

```
field->cName := "Paul"
```

The second way is to use the **replace** command this has the advantage of being able to alter the contents of more than one field at a time.

```
REPLACE cName WITH "Paul",cTel WITH "0815894499"
```

will replace the value in the field cName with 'Paul' and the value in cTel with '0815894499'. Note if there is an index active when you modify the key fields the records relative position in the file may change although it will still be the current record.

Field

In the above section it was mentioned that a field can be treated like a variable if it is preceded by an alias, however this alias can be omitted if the alias has previously been declared. This declaration is done with the **field** command, fields declared using the **field** command have the same scopping as static variables.

```
FIELD cName, cAdd1, cAdd2
```

will state that cName, cAdd1, and cAdd2 are fields in the current file. It is also possible to state which file the fields are in by using the **in** keyword

```
FIELD cName, cAdd1, cAdd2 IN customer
```

will state that these fields can be found in the file whose alias is customer irrelevant of which file is in the currently active workarea.

Delete, recall, pack, zap, reindex

Having added records there is usually a need to delete some of them, in CA-Clipper this is again a two stage process. First a record can be marked for deletion, this is done with the **delete** command which will mark the current record for deletion. Once done it is possible to remove this mark using the **recall** command, and using the **deleted()** function it is possible to detect the delete status of the current record. When called this function returns true if the current record is marked for deletion and false if it is not.

```
DELETE
? deleted()
RECALL
? deleted()
```

the above piece of code will first display .T. followed by .F. indicating the status of the record. Once a large number of records have been marked for deletion there will be a large amount of wasted space in the file. This space can be recovered using the **pack** command. Once this command has been issued the records marked for deletion will have been removed and therefore can not be recalled. To delete all the records in the file you can either add the keyword **all** to the command **delete** and then pack the file or you can use the command **zap** which will perfom the same function but is much faster. If an index is not consistent with its file (perhaps due to the file being packed with the index closed) it can be rebuilt by issuing the **reindex** command. This command will cause all indexes open in the current workarea to be rebuilt.

Note

As reindexing the file will not work if the file header on the index file is corrupt it is often preferable to recreate the index using **index on**.

Seek, skip, go

Having created a file complete with indexes, and then having added records to that file, we now need a method of finding the desired record. The **seek** command gives you a way of using the current index so that

```
USE customer INDEX name, invoice
SEEK "Paul"
```

will search the index for the key 'Paul'. If it is found the function **found()** will return a value of true and the record pointer will point to the desired record. Having finished with this record we will want to move to another. If we know the position of our next record in relation to the current one, we can use the **skip** command. Skip allows you to move the record pointer a desired number of records by placing the required number after the command. If this number is missing skip will move 1 record down the file in the order of the current index. If the next record has been deleted and **set delete** is on (set delete is used to tell CA-Clipper to ignore deleted records) skip will not count this record and move again.

```
SKIP
```

will move the record pointer 1 place down the file

```
SKIP -5
```

will move the record pointer 5 places up the file. If you know the number of the required record it is possible to go directly to it using the **go** command.

```
GO 5
```

will move the pointer to the fifth record in the file (provided there are at least 5 records in the file). It is also possible to jump to the beginning or end of the file by using the commands **go top** and **go bottom** respectively. If there is a filter active (see later) these commands will move the pointer to the beginning or end of the scoped records.

Set softseek

If a seek fails to find the desired record, the record pointer will be placed in one of two places depending on the setting of softseek. If softseek is 'off' the record pointer will be at the end of the file however, if it is 'on', the current record will be the one with the smallest key which is greater than the one sought.

Dbseek()

The actions of **seek**, **softseek**, and **found()** are all combined in the function dbseek(). This function accepts two parameters, the first is the key to be sought, and the second which is optional is the setting of softseek. This parameter is a logical and can be set to .T. for 'on' or .F. for 'off', if omitted the current 'global' setting of softseek is used. When called this function will return a logical value to indicate whether it was successful (in the same way as a subsequent call to found() will).

Locate, continue

If the current file does not have an appropriate index open the desired record can still be found by using the locate command. Locate is much slower than seek but can also be much more versatile. The locate command has three parameters of which only the second is required.

```
LOCATE FOR cName = "Paul"
```

will start at the beginning of the file and find the first record which contains 'Paul' in the field cName. This expression can be extended using the `.and.` & `.or.` operators. It is also possible to add a 'while' scope to this command.

```
LOCATE FOR cName = "Paul" WHILE cPost = "BS1"
```

This will search for the same record however this time if it encounters a post code with a value other than 'BS1' it will exit leaving **found()** set to false. Once a record is found it is possible to move to the next record which matches the expression by using the continue command. The **continue** command has one deficiency in that it does not adhere to any while clause, if a while clause is to be used the **continue** command can be replaced with the **locate** command combined with the **rest** keyword. Used in this way the **locate** command will search the file starting with the current record, it is therefore necessary to move to the next record before issuing this command.

```
SKIP
LOCATE REST FOR cName = "Paul" WHILE cPost = "BS1"
```

will therefore continue the above **locate** command.

Bof(), eof(), recno()

There are three functions which are of great use when navigating a file, these are **bof()** which returns true if an attempt is made to move past the beginning of the file (i.e. skip -1 from the first record), **eof()** which returns true if an attempt is made to move past the end of the file, and **recno()** which returns the number of the current record.

Set filter

Set filter can be used to hide records which do not meet a required condition, the filter will not be active until the record pointer is moved

```
SET FILTER TO left(cPost, 2) == "BS"
GO TOP
```

this will cause only those records whose postcode starts with the letters 'BS' to be visible, and places the record pointer at the first record in the scope. It is not necessary that the fields in the expression are in the index, indeed filters can be used on files which do not have any indexes open.

Set relation

If two files contain data which is related, CA-Clipper will allow you to link these files, by using **set relation** it is possible to link a parent file to up to eight child files. Before a child file can be linked to the parent it must have an active index, this index is then used to perform a **seek** in the child each time the record pointer moves in the parent. If invoice is a file containing invoice numbers

```
USE customer INDEX invoice NEW
USE invoice NEW
SET RELATION TO nNumber INTO customer
DO WHILE !eof()
   ? customer->cName + " " + str(nNumber)
   SKIP
ENDDO
```

will display the number of each invoice and the name of the customer to which it was sent in the order of the records in the invoice file. **Set relation** clears all relations for which the current workarea is the parent. If you wish to add a relation to those already active in the current workarea add the keyword **additive** to the statement.

Count, sum

A major part of many systems is statistics. It is of course possible to skip through the file counting each occurrence of records in which an expression evaluates to true. If the records have numeric fields, these can be summed in the same way. These two processes can be replaced with the commands **count** and **sum**, these commands both have *for* and *while* clauses which behave in the same way as those in the **locate** command

```
nCount := 0
nSum   := 0
COUNT TO nCount FOR cName = "Paul"
SUM nInvoice TO nSum FOR cName = "Paul"
```

the above will assign to the variable nCount the number of records which contain 'Paul' in the field cName it will then sum the field nInvoice in the aforementioned records and assign this value to the variable nSum.

Copy to

Using the **copy to** command it is possible to copy part or all of a data file to a second file which can either be another data file or a text file. This command always creates a new file and if it is merelyfollowed by a filename will make a copy of the file in the current work area. While this is of use this command really comes into it's own when you start adding parameters to it, firstly you can specify the fields you wish to copy by listing them after the keyword **fields**, next you can add **while** and **for** clauses which limit the records to be copied. If a while clause is added all records from the current record will be copied until the condition fails, and if a for clause is used only those records which match the condition will be copied. These clauses can of course be used together.

```
USE customer
COPY FIELDS cAdd1, cAdd2 TO temp FOR left(cPost, 2) = "BS"
```

will open the customer file, create a new file called temp.dbf and copy into it the address fields for each record whose postcode starts with "BS". There is one more parameter which can be added to this command and that alters the output file format, if the letters **sdf** are added to the command the output will be in System Data Format which is fixed length records with each field separated by a space. A third output format can be specified by using the keyword **delimited** which caulses all fields to be separated by commas and text fields to be surounded by double quotes. The character which is used to suround text fields can be changed by following the delimited keyword by **with** and the character to be used (enclosed in quotes).

```
USE customer
COPY TO temp DELIMITED WITH "'"
```

will copy the contents of the customer file to temp.txt, separate each field with a comma and surround each text field with single quotes.

Append from

This command is the opposite of copy to, it is used to copy data into the current file. It uses the same parameters as copy to.

Warning

If the source and current files both contain a field with the same name, this field must be of the same type or an error will occur.

Set printer to

We have already seen how to print directly to the printer using **set printer on** however it is often desirable to write to a text file and then print this file at a later date. This can be achieved using the **set printer to** command followed by the name of the file to be created. Once this command has been issued you should print in the normal way and to close the file simply re-issue the command without a filename.

Fcreate()

We have so far seen how to use data files and how to create text files, the remainder of the functions covered in this chapter will enable you to access any type of file for which you know the structure. The first of the functions is **fcreate()** which as it's name suggests creates a new file, it accepts two parameters of which the first is the name of the file to be created and the second (if passed) is the attribute to be applied to the file when it is closed. This function returns a file handle which is a number between 0 and 65535 if the file has been created otherwise it returns -1, this file handle should be stored as it is required each time the file is accessed. Below is a list of the attributes which can be applied to the file.

Value	*Attribute*	*Description*
0	Normal	Create a read/write file
1	Read only	Create a read only file
2	Hidden	Create a hidden file
4	System	Create a system file

Fopen()

If the file already exists it can be opened using the **fopen()** function. This function accepts the filename as the first parameter and if required a second parameter to indicate the mode in which it is to be used. If the file is only to be read a value of 0 should be passed (this can be omitted), if it is to be written to, a value of 1 should be used, and if both actions are to be performed use a value of 2. When called fopen() returns a file handle (see above).

Fwrite()

Having opened/created your file you will need to write to it, this is done using the **fwrite()** function. This function requires the file handle (returned when the file was opened) and a character string containing the data to be written, it can also accept a third parameter which is the number of characters to be written from the string (if omitted the complete string will be used). Fwrite() will return the number of characters it has written meaning that if this number is not equal to the number required an error has occurred.

Fread()

You can now open a file and write to it, the next thing to do is read from it. This can be done with the **fread()** function which requires three parameters, the first is the handle of the file to be read from, the second is a character string into which the data should be placed, and the third is the number of characters to be read (this should not be greater than the length of the character string). Fread() returns the number of characters read and hence if this is less then the third parameter an error has occurred. Once a number of characters have been read from a file the file pointer is positioned at the next character to be read.

Note

As the data is to be placed at the address of the character string, the parameter should be passed by reference (prefaced with an @).

Fseek()

We are now able to read data from the current position in the file however we would be very lucky indeed if this was always the data we required. It is far more likely that we would need to move the file pointer first, and this can be done with the fseek() function. This function requires the file handle, and the number of characters to move the pointer relative to one of three positions in the file, these positions are dictated by the third parameter. If this parameter contains the value 0 (or is not passed) the pointer will be moved from the begining of the file, if the value is 2 the pointer will be moved from the end of the file, but if the value is 1 the pointer will be moved in relation to its current position. If the second parameter is positive the pointer will be moved forward through the file and if negative it will go backwards.

Fclose()

Having created/opened a file read from it and written to it all that now remains to be done to it is close it. This can be done with the fclose() function which simply accepts the handle of the file to be closed and returns a logical value to indicate whether or not it was successful.

Summary

In this chapter you have seen how to access files (both data and text). You have seen how to create them, how to read from and write to them, and how they can be closed. You have also seen how to search through them although this has a slightly different meaning with text files.

Problems

5.1 Lastkey() *will equal 27 if the last key pressed was escape. Using this function and the customer file which was created in this chapter write a program which accepts customer details and writes them to the file. The program should exit when escape is pressed.*

5.2 *Write a program which accepts a customer's name and displays their address.*

5.3 *Write a program which opens the file* c:\autoexec.bat *and displays its contents on the screen.*

6 Tables and code blocks

One of the things which seems to characterize most CA-Clipper programs is the inclusion of a large number of tables. These tables can be used to display everything from files to menus. In this chapter you will see how to create some of these tables, you will be introduced to two of the classes which come with CA-Clipper and in order that you should be able to use them you will discover the power of code blocks.

Achoice()

Achoice() is used to browse arrays, however as it was not re-written for version 5 it is only able to handle single dimension arrays. It can also be used for bounce bar menus, indeed according to the manuals this is its prime use although it is far more powerful than is required for most menus of this type. The first five parameters are mandatory, they are the coordinates of the top left and bottom right corners of the browse window and the array of character strings which are to be browsed

```
achoice(5,5,15,25,aNames)
```

will enable you to browse the array aNames in a window between rows 5 and 15 and columns 5 and 25. If a name is selected by pressing return **achoice()** will return its array position, if selection is aborted by pressing escape it will return 0. When called in this fashion each key is processed in the following manner.

Key	***Description***
Up arrow	Move up one line
Down arrow	Move down one line
Home/Ctrl PgUp	Move to the first item in the array

Key	***Description***
End/Ctrl PgDn	Move to the last item in the array
PgUp	Move up one page
PgDn	Move down one page
Return	Select item
Esc/Left arrow/ Right arrow	Abort selection
Letter	Move to the next item beginning with letter

The rest of the parameters are used to tailor the way **achoice()** behaves. The first is an array of logical values one for each element in the browse array to state whether or not each item is selectable; if an item is not it is merely skipped during the browse. This array can be replaced by a single logical value which would then apply to all the items. If no item is selectable then the browse will immediately exit. Next is the name of a user function (see later), followed by the numbers of the item to be highlighted when **achoice()** is entered and the row on which it should be displayed. It should be noted that **achoice()** cannot be used to browse empty arrays, similarly **achoice()** will only display the array it is passed so that if your function adds or deletes elements to or from the array **achoice()** must be exited and re-entered before they will be seen.

User function

This function is called when there are no selectable items, when there are no keys to process, when a key has been pressed which **achoice()** doesn't know how to handle, and when an attempt has been made to move past the beginning or end of the array. When called this function is passed three values, these are the current mode, the number of the currently highlighted element and the relative row position of this element within the window.

This function returns a value to instruct **achoice()** how to behave. If the function returns a value of 0 **achoice()** will abort with a value of 0, if 1 is returned **achoice()** will exit with the number of the element selected. A value of 2 will continue the browse and a value of 3 will highlight the next element which starts with the key pressed. The values of the mode parameter are:

Mode	*Description*
0	Idle
1	Attempt to pass the beginning of the array
2	Attempt to pass the end of the array
3	Keystroke exception
4	No selectable items

Code blocks

Code blocks are a feature introduced in version 5 to in-order that you can add functionality to the pre-defined classes however their use goes much further than this. A **code block** is a piece of code which when evaluated returns a value, valid blocks of code are therefore expressions and function calls, (commands and statements do not return values and therefore are not valid in code blocks). If more than one expression is included in the block (separated by commas), all the expressions will be evaluated (from left to right) but only the value of the last one will be returned. The feature which distinguishes code blocks from other blocks of code is the fact that they are held in variables and therefore can be passed to functions in the same way as any other parameter. To define a piece of code as a code block it should be surrounded by curly braces ({}) and immediately inside the opening brace should be placed two vertical bars (||). If the code within the block uses values which are to be passed as parameters, the variables into which these parameters are to be placed should be listed between the vertical bars. To evaluate a code block it should be passed along with any parameters to the **eval()** function. A simple but effective method of demonstrating code blocks is the replacement of the following functions

```
FUNCTION nMultiply(nFirst, nSecond)
RETURN (nFirst * nSecond)

FUNCTION nAdd(nFirst, nSecond)
RETURN (nFirst + nSecond)
```

when called the first function will return the value of `nFirst` multiplied by `nSecond`, and the second will return `nFirst` plus `nSecond`

```
nMultiply := {|nFirst, nSecond|nFirst * nSecond}
nAdd      := {|nFirst, nSecond|nFirst + nSecond}

FUNCTION nMaths(nFirst, nSecond, bProcess)
RETURN eval(bProcess, nFirst, nSecond)
```

the previous two functions have now been replaced with the function `nMaths()` which is passed the two values on which to perform the equation and the equation itself. This may not seem to be much of an improvement over the first method but consider how each method could implement the processes of divide and subtract. As code blocks are held in variables they can be returned from functions and then be used in other parts of your program, however as code blocks can refer to local variables which are in scope at the time they are created we are presented with a problem namely what happens to the local variable when the function returns (normally it would be destroyed). The answer is that the variable becomes what is known as a detached local and remains in existence (and in scope) until the code block is destroyed.

Aeval()

If a code block is to be evaluated on a number of elements from the same array it is often better to use the **aeval()** function. This function accepts the array to which a code block is to be applied, the code block to apply, the number of the element to start with (if not passed aeval() will start with element 1), and the number of elements to be processed (if not passed all elements will be processed). The code block is passed two parameters the first being the value of the current element and the second the position of the current element in the array.

```
LOCAL aArray[6]
aeval(aArray,{|cVal,nPoss| if((nPoss % 2) = 0, ;
     aArray[nPos] := "Even", aArray[nPos] := "Odd")})
```

will declare an array of 6 elements and then place the string “Even” elements 2, 4, 6 and the string “Odd” in elements 1, 3, 5.

Dbeval()

Just as **aeval()** applies a code block to an array **dbeval()** will apply a code block to the current data file. It requires the code block to be applied and is optionally followed by a code block which must evaluate to true for the process to be applied (a for clause), a code block which terminates dbeval() as soon as it results in false (a while clause), the number of records to be processed, the number of the record to be processed, and a logical value to indicate whether to start from the current record or from the start of the file.

Note

None of the code blocks used in this function are passed any parameters and dbeval() does not return a value.

Tbrowse

CA-Clipper 5 is a semi object oriented language in that it has several pre-defined classes, the first of which is the tbrowse which is in fact two classes one to handle the table and the other to handle individual columns. A tbrowse table consists of two parts, the browse mechanism and the columns. A table is created using either of the **tbrowsenew()** or the **tbrowsedb()** functions, and columns are created using the **tbcolumnnew()** function. In the following pages we shall create a tbrowse to browse the customer file that we created in chapter 5, and show you how to create other tables to browse subsets of data. It is not our intention to tell you everything about tbrowse but by the end of this chapter you should be able to create simple tables and have an idea as to how they can be enhanced. First, we must create the tbrowse object:

```
USE customer
oBrowse := TBrowseDB(1, 1, 20, 60)
```

The above will create an empty table called oBrowse which will be displayed in a window between the coordinates 1,1 and 20,60. You should be aware that as we have not yet defined the contents of the table, we did not need the file to be open however it needs to be opened somewhere and the start is as good a place as any. Notice that we used the function **tbrowsedb()** and not **tbrowsenew()**, either would have done the job, however by using the former CA-Clipper will have created three methods for us. These methods (which will only work on files) move to the beginning of the file, move to the end of the file, and move to the next record within the file. To add a new column to the table it must first be created using the **tbcolumnnew()** function and then added to the table using the addcolumn method. This can be done as a one or two stage process, **tbcolumnnew()** accepts two parameters, the first is the column title and the second is a code block which returns the data to be displayed on the current line in the column

```
oBrowse:addColumn(TBColumnNew("Name",{||cName}))
oBrowse:addColumn(TBColumnNew("Add1",{||cAdd1}))
oBrowse:addColumn(TBColumnNew("Add2",{||cAdd2}))
oBrowse:addColumn(TBColumnNew("Post",{||cPost}))
oBrowse:addColumn(TBColumnNew("Tel",{||cTel}))
oBrowse:addColumn(TBColumnNew("Invoice",{||nInvoice}))
```

The above will create a column for each field in the file and add them to the table. We are now in a position to write the browse. The first thing we must do is to display our table, this is done by calling the **stabilize()** method. This method will draw part of the table each time it is called and should be called repeatedly until it returns a value of true indicating that the table is stable. Once the table has been drawn you should wait for a key to be pressed whereupon you can take the appropriate action.

```
nKey := 0
DO WHILE nKey != 27
   DO WHILE !oBrowse:Stabilize()
   ENDDO
   nKey := inkey(0)
   DO CASE
   CASE nKey == 5
      oBrowse:up()
```

```
   CASE nKey == 24
      oBrowse:down()
   CASE nKey == 4
      oBrowse:right()
   CASE nKey == 19
      oBrowse:left()
   ENDCASE
ENDDO
```

The above loop will perform a simple browse on our table, it uses the arrow keys to move between fields and exits when the escape key is pressed. Below is a list of all the movement methods which can be used in a table.

Method	***Description***
down()	move down one row
end()	move to the right-most visible column
gobottom()	go to the end of the table
gotop()	go to the beginning of the table
home()	move to the left-most visible column
left()	move left one column
pageup()	move up one page
pagedown()	move down one page
panend()	move to the right-most column
panhome()	move to the left-most column
panleft()	pan the table to the left keeping the current column highlighted if possible
panright()	Pan the table to the right keeping the current column highlighted if possible
right()	move right one column
up()	move up one row

GoTopBlock, GoBottomBlock

As has already been mentioned tbrowsedb() creates methods the first two of which are goTopBlock and goBottomBlock (the third is skipBlock see later). These contain code blocks to move to the begining and end of the data respectively, however they are only required if you intend to use the gotop() and gobottom() movement methods.

```
USE customer
oBrowse := TBrowseNew(1, 1, 20, 60)
oBrowse:goTopBlock    := {||dbgotop()}
oBrowse:goBottomBlock := {||dbgobottom()}
```

will create a tbrowse with the same functionality to the one previously created with tbrowsedb (with the exception of the skipblock see later). As you can see these code blocks are quite simple and it is therefore quite easy (if you have an active index) to simulate a filter by changing these to seek for the desired record for the goTopBlock and seek for the next key followed by a dbskip(-1) for the goBottomBlock. This method of applying a filter is much faster than **set filter to**.

SkipBlock

The skipBlock is slightly more complicated in that it is the routine which performs the movement between rows in the table. It is passed the number of rows to move (positive for down, negative for up) and returns the number of rows it was possible to move. These two numbers will be different if an attempt is made to move beyond the beginning or end of the data.

```
oBrowse:skipBlock := {|nRec|nSkipBlock(nRec)}

FUNCTION nSkipBlock(nRec)

    LOCAL nMoved := 0, nDirection
    IF nRec == 0
        SKIP 0
    ELSE
        IF nRec > 0
            nDirection := 1
        ELSE
```

```
            nDirection := -1
        ENDIF
        DO WHILE nMoved != nRec .and. !eof() .and. !bof()
            SKIP nDirection
            nMoved ++
        ENDDO
        DO CASE
            CASE eof() .and. nMoved != 0
                SKIP -1
                nMoved --
            CASE bof() .and. nMoved != 0
                GOTO recno() // clears bof() without
                nMoved ++    // moving the record pointer
        ENDCASE
    ENDIF
RETURN nMoved
```

is the skipblock missing from the above tbrowse, the skip 0 is required to refresh the current row in the event that it changed. As you can see the work is done by a DO WHILE loop which detects when the boundaries of the data have been reached, it would therefore be a simple matter to add further conditions to implement a filter. The case statement is simply to move the record pointer back into the file if it is moved past one of the ends. If end of file is true the record pointer will point to a phantom record at the end of the file however if beginning of file is true the current record will still be the first record in the file meaning that to clear the flag the pointer must be moved without changing the record number.

RefreshCurrent(), refreshAll()

Tbrowse operates on a buffered set of data and hence if you change the data you can easily get into the position where the data you are looking at is out of date. This can be prevented by issuing either the refreshCurrent() or the refreshAll() method which cause tbrowse to re-read either the current row or all rows respectively during the next stabilize.

Summary

In this chapter you saw how to browse single dimension arrays using achoice(). You also saw how to write code blocks and then in the sections on tbrowse you saw many examples of how they are used. The sections on tbrowse first showed you how to create a simple table, it then went on to show you the code which had been generated for you and how by writing it yourself you could create a table to browse a subset of the data and in the exercises at the end of the chapter you will be asked to create a tbrowse for an array.

Problems

6.1 Write the code blocks to implement the divide and subtract processes for use in the function nMaths() *above.*

6.2 Write an achoice() *which starts with one name and allows you to add more. When the function is exited it should state how it finished and which element if any was selected.*

6.3 Improve the above first tbrowse *so that it also displays the fields from the related file invoice also mentioned in chapter 5.*

6.4 Write a function which creates a tbrowse *which will browse an array passed to it as a parameter. You will have to use* tbrowsenew *and write your own* gotopblock, gobottomblock, *and* skipblock.

7 Help, get and error systems

In this chapter you will see how to create help and error handling routines. How to get more out of the get system including how to write your own get readers, and will also see a new special type of function called a 'get/set function'. The get and error systems are the last two classes supplied with CA-Clipper whereas the facilities for providing help are more primitive and therefore require more effort if the results are to be of note.

Help

The amount of help provided by your system is limited only by the amount of work you as a programmer are prepared to put into writing it; it can range from none (at its simplest) to full context sensitive help giving several relevant examples at any time. Whilst an extensive help system can involve a lot of work there are ways of reducing this by using code generators or by storing the screens in data files.

Set key 28 to help

The simplest help systems are merely menu options which, when selected display text on the screen. While systems of this nature have their place they are so easy to write (and indeed are no different from any other function you have already written) that we shall not investigate them any further here preferring instead to use **set key** to provide a more event driven system. In chapter 4 we mentioned that (unless redefined) all CA-Clipper systems have the F1 key so defined that when it is pressed in a wait state a call is made to the procedure **Help**, unfortunately as CA-Clipper does not pre-define this procedure unless you write it yourself pressing F1 will have no effect. When the F1 key is pressed during a wait state the help procedure (or function) is passed three parameters, these are the name of the calling procedure, the number of the line that was being executed and the name of the variable that was being read. A combination of these parameters can be used to determine not only where the program was when the key was pressed but also what it was doing. Although it is not possible to state which combination will be the most efficient as this largely depends on the individual program, as a general rule the line number is the least helpful.

```
FUNCTION Help(cName, nLine, cVar)

  DO CASE
    CASE cVar = "CNAME"
     @ 0, 24 SAY "Enter name"
    CASE left(cVar, 4) = "CFADD" .or. cVar = "CFPOST"
     @ 0, 24 SAY "Enter the first address"
    CASE cVar = "LSECOND"
     @ 0, 24 SAY "Enter 'Y' if there is a second address"
    CASE left(cVar, 4) = "CSADD" .or. cVar = "CSPOST"
     @ 0, 24 SAY "Enter the second address"
  ENDCASE
  inkey(0)
  @ 0, 24 SAY "                                              "
RETURN
```

If the above were to be included with the function GetTest from chapter 3 it would provide a context sensitive help message on line 24 each time the F1 key is pressed. While this is a very simple example, it does show two very important points: the first is the general structure of a hard coded help function and the second is that for a large system a function of this nature would be very costly in both time and effort to produce. A different approach would be to hold the help screens in a data file and simply use the help function to display them. This could be the first step towards writing a code generator to produce the final function or, the combination of the data file and the function could be included in your final system, this would give the added benefit that if a help screen needed changing you would only have to change the data in the file, the program would remain the same and would not therefore require re-compiling.

Name	***Type***	***Size***
NAME	C	10
LINE	N	10
VAR	C	10
TOPROW	N	2
TOPCOL	N	2
BOTROW	N	2
BOTCOL	N	2
TEXT	M	10

if the above file were created with the name Help and indexed on the expression

```
NAME + str(LINE) + VAR
```

the following function would search for some text and if found would display it

```
FUNCTION Help(cName, nLine, cVar)

  LOCAL nArea := select()
  LOCAL cScreen
  USE help INDEX help NEW
  IF dbseek(cName + str(nLine) + cVar)
    cScreen := savescreen(toprow, topcol, botrow, botcol)
    dispbox(toprow, topcol, botrow, botcol, "╔═╗║╝═╚║ ")
    memoedit(text, toprow + 1, topcol + 1, botrow - 1, ;
             botcol - 1, .f.)
    inkey(0)
    restscreen(toprow, topcol, botrow, botcol, cScreen)
  ENDIF
```

```
  CLOSE
  select(nArea)
RETURN nil
```

this is a fairly basic function however it would not take much to add fields to the file to dictate the characters used to draw the box and the colours in which the screen should be displayed.

Get/Set functions

These are functions which behave like variables in that they allow access to a value. When called the function will return the value contained in the variable however if a parameter is passed then the variable is updated to contain the new value.

```
FUNCTION nGetSet(nValue)
  STATIC nVar
  IF nValue != nil
    nVar := nValue
  ENDIF
RETURN nVar
```

the variable nVar is only in scope within the function nGetSet however as it is declared as a static its value is retained between calls. The function always returns the current value of nVar in effect causing it to be in scope anywhere and if a value is passed to the function then nVar is assigned this value. One of the advantages of a function of this type is that it is possible to prevent the variable being assigned a value of the wrong type or outside a desired range. Another advantage is that the function could be placed in a codeblock provided the variable is declared outside.

```
STATIC nVar
nGetSet := {|nValue|if(nValue != nil, nVar := nValue, ;
                  nValue}
```

the codeblock above would behave the same as the previous function. An example of a function of this type is the **setcolor()** function.

The Get system

We have already seen that you don't have to use the get system to use gets however this is not actually correct as the pre-processor (see later) converts each get statement into a call to the get system meaning that we have already seen one method of using this system.

```
@ 1, 0 GET nVar WHEN nVar > 10 PICTURE "999" ;
            VALID nVar < 100
```

is converted into the following function calls

```
setpos(1, 0)
aadd(GetList, _GET_(nVar, "nVar", "999", {||nVar < 100},;
              {||nVar > 10})
```

as has been mentioned previously each get is held in a public array called GetList, in the example this can be seen by the fact that aadd() is used to place the result of the function _get_() in the array GetList, the result of this function is a get object and so GetList is an array of get objects. From the example we also see that _get_() is a constructor function for the get system however as Computer Associates do not guarantee that functions which begin with an underscore will remain in the same form in any future release and, should therefore not be used we need another constructor function. The other function is called GetNew()

GetNew()

GetNew() returns an empty get object in which each of the instance variables must then be set, however some of them can be set by passing them as parameters. The first two are the row and column positions of the get, the third is a get/set codeblock used to assign to the variable

Following these are three character strings containing the name of the variable being edited, the picture string, and the colour string. Once the object has been created the values in these instance variables along with those listed below can be changed.

Name	***Description***
Block	The get/set codeblock (see above).
Buffer	This is where the value is edited.
Cargo	This is used to hold any data that you wish to include in the object.
Changed	A logical stating whether the value has been changed since the get was entered.
Clear	A logical value indicating whether or not to clear the buffer at the start of editing.
Col	The column position of the get.
Colorspec	The colours to be used by the get (if not set the global settings are used).
Exitstate	A numeric used to indicate what method was used to leave the get.
Minus	A logical indicating whether or not a minus sign is in the buffer.
Name	This is the string returned from readvar() (this is the value passed to any function called from set key).
Picture	The picture string used to format the editing.
Pos	The position of any decimal point in a numeric get.
Postblock	A codeblock containing the valid clause. When called the get system passes the get object to this codeblock.
Preblock	A codeblock containing the when clause. When called the get system passes the get object to this codeblock.

Name	*Description*
Reader	A codeblock containing a customized function used to perform the get (see readmodal()).
Row	The row position of the get.

```
oGet     := getnew()
oGet:row := 10
```

shows how the instance variables can be set. One of the major differences between _get_() and getnew() is that when an object is created using _get_() it is displayed whereas to do this with getnew() the method display() must be used.

```
oGet:display()
```

will therefore display the get we created earlier (although it would first need its other instance variables set).

Readmodal()

It has already been said that gets are not activated until a read is issued however as we have shown that get commands are calls to the get system you may be wondering how the read command relates to the system. When this command is compiled it is converted into a call to **readmodal()**, we have already seen that the get objects are stored in the array GetList, this array is passed to readmodal() as a parameter and if the keyword **save** does not follow the read command this array is then emptied. We have seen how to create get objects and store them in our own array it is therefore reasonable to assume that any array of get objects could be passed to readmodal(). This is not only the case but is often desirable when writing systems where the same input screens are to be used more than once. If we had two get object arrays called oScreen1 and oScreen2

```
aeval(oScreen1,{|oGet|oGet:display()})
readmodal(oScreen1)
aeval(oScreen2,{|oGet|oGet:display()})
readmodal(oScreen2)
aeval(oScreen1,{|oGet|oGet:display()})
readmodal(oScreen1)
```

will cause the first set of gets to be edited, once finished the second set will be edited and on completion the first set will be returned to.

Reader

As we have seen gets are edited using the readmodal() function. This is a CA-Clipper function the source code for which comes with CA-Clipper (in getsys.prg) and can therefore be changed. This is not a task which should be taken lightly as although it is not difficult it does require a detailed knowledge of how the get system works. A simpler method of altering the behaviour of the get system (especially if it should only be different for one or two gets) is to use the **reader** instance variable. If you look though the code for readmodal() you will notice that if the reader instance variable contains a codeblock then this block is evaluated and if not a call to getreader() is made. The purpose of these functions is to control the editing of the individual gets and to return when an exit key is pressed (an exit key is any key which causes you to leave the get such as return or up arrow) in order that any keystrokes can be applied to the get, the object is passed as a parameter to the function. In **getreader()** there is a call to the function **getapplykey()** whose job it is to process the input. It is passed the get object and the value of the key that was pressed and is simply a very large case statement whereby the keys can be identified and applied. In order that you can better understand how this variable can be used we will now write a reader which will enable you to increment/ decrement a date field using the page up/page down keys this can be done by making a copy of the getreader() function called datereader() in which the call to getapplykey() is replaced with a similar call to dateapplykey() which is shown below. This function uses the function transform() which takes a value and a picture string as parameters and returns a string containing the formatted value. It also uses the method **untransform()** which returns the value in the objects buffer in its original type. The rest of the methods used have been kept to a minimum for the sake of clarity, however once you are happy with the way it works you can add more to increase its functionality.

```
FUNCTION DateReader(oGet, nKey)

    LOCAL dDate
    DO CASE
        CASE nKey == 5
            oGet:exitstate := 1
        CASE nKey == 24
            oGet:exitstate := 2
        CASE nKey == 13
            oGet:exitstate := 5
        CASE nKey == 27 .and. set(_set_escape)
            oGet:undo()
            oGet:exitstate := 7
        CASE nKey == 18
            dDate := oGet:unTransform()
            dDate += 1
            oGet:buffer := transform(dDate, oGet:picture)
        CASE nKey == 3
            dDate := oGet:unTransform()
            dDate -= 1
```

```
            oGet:buffer := transform(dDate, oGet:picture)
   ENDCASE
   oGet:display()
RETURN
```

This reader can be applied by setting the reader variable to the codeblock

```
{|oGet|DateReader(oGet)}
```

Error handling

There are two approaches to error handling – prevention and cure. We have already covered prevention in the form of picture strings and valid functions for gets which prevent the wrong type of input and values outside of any acceptable ranges. Prevention also comes in the form of program design, an example of which is ensuring that a variable does not contain zero before it is used in division. Cure is more difficult due to the fact that you have to predict what errors will arise, and by their very nature errors are things which cannot be predicted. However there are some places in a program where certain errors are predictable and can therefore be trapped; examples of these are DOS errors when accessing data, and passing the wrong types of variables to a function. The action your program takes when an error occurs is up to you as the programmer, the easiest is to stop the program and exit to DOS however while this is necessary for some errors it is a little drastic when the error is as simple as there not being a disk in the drive or the printer not being switched on. There are three types of error recovery, the first is to design your program to check for each error at each point where it is likely to arise. This is impractical for most errors however it does have a place when something must happen before you can continue (such as the printer being turned on). The second is to use sequences which we cover next, and the third is to use the error system which will conclude this chapter.

Begin sequence

Sequences are areas of a program which perform discreet tasks and in which if an error occurs normal processing should cease and remedial action be taken. A sequence is delimited by the commands **begin sequence** and **end**. If there are remedial actions which should take place they are placed before the **end** keyword and separated from the rest of the sequence by the keyword **recover** (or **recover using** if a parameter is to be received). If during the processing of a sequence the function **break()** is encountered processing immediately jumps to the first line after the end (or recover if it exists). If a parameter is passed to the recovery routine it is normally an error object, however its type is not defined and can therefore be anything to help with the recovery. In the main block of a sequence you should not use the commands **return** or **loop** as return will exit the function the sequence is in and loop will restart the sequence, however they can be used as part of the recovery routine. An example sequence can be found in appendix D.

Note

Return and loop should not be used in the body of a sequence but can be used in a recovery routine.

Error class

Unlike the other classes we have met the error class has instance variables but no methods and as such is merely a method of holding a collection of information about the routing in which the error occurred. When an error occurs an error object is created and passed to the current error handling routine which then uses it to decide on which action to take.

Errorblock()

When an error occurs an error object is passed to the current error handler. This handler is defined by the **errorblock()** function. The handler is passed as a parameter in the form of a codeblock which accepts an error object as a parameter of its own. This handler once 'posted' has global scope and therefore stays active until it is replaced by another. When errorblock() is called it returns the previous handler so that it may be stored and if desired later restored. By placing a call to this handler it is also possible to chain handlers together so that new handlers merely enhance the actions of the error system rather than replacing them altogether.

```
oOldHandler := errorblock({|oErr|MyHandler(oErr), ;
                         eval(oOldHandler, oErr)})
```

when an error occurs the function call above will pass MyHandler() the error object. Once MyHandler() has finished the object is then passed to the previous handler so that it may (if it wishes) also take action.

```
errorblock({|oErr|break(oErr)})
```

if the above handler were in force during a sequence and an error occurred, processing would immediately jump to the recovery section passing it the error object.

> **Note**
>
> Errorblock() is a get/set function, meaning that a copy of the current handler can be retrieved simply by calling this function without a parameter.

Errornew()

This is the object creation function for the error class. You might think that as an error object is created whenever a CA-Clipper detects an error you do not need a function of this type, however there are some types of errors which can occur in a program which are application dependent and which CA-Clipper can have no way of detecting, an example of this is when two columns of figures should tally. When called this function returns an empty error object in which you should assign each of the instance variables which are applicable, a list of the instance variables is below. Once the variables have been assigned the error system can be called using the command

```
eval(errorblock(), oErrorObject)
```

where oErrorObject is your own error object.

args	an array of the parameters passed to the operator or function in which the error occurred.
candefault	contains T if the calling routine can perform a default recovery action.
canretry	contains T if the calling routine can retry the operation.
cansubstitute	contains T if the calling routine can substitute a value and continue.
cargo	a variable containing anything you wish to put in it.

description	a character description of the error.
filename	the name of the file involved in the error (only some systems use this).
gencode	a numeric value indicating the error.
operation	the name of the operation or function in which the error occurred.
oscode	the operating system error code (only used if the error is an operating system error).
severity	a number indicating the severity of the error.
subcode	a value indicating the subsystem error code if available.
subsystem	the name of the subsystem in which the error occurred.
tries	the number of times a retry has been attempted.

A default, retry, or substitution is requested by the handler returning a value of true.

Note

candefault, canretry and cansubstitute are mutually exclusive. Meaning that if one is set to true the others must be set to false.

Summary

In this chapter we have seen how to create help screens and how to achieve greater control over user input with the use of get readers. We have also seen how to approach the difficult area of error handling with the use of both sequences and the error system.

Problems

7.1 Write a routine which allows you to modify the data held in HELP.DBF or if no record is found, create a new screen. It should allow you to enter the coordinates of the screen, edit the text and save details.

7.2 Modify DateReader so that control page up/page down change the month and alt page up/page down change the year.

8 Further ideas

Using the information presented in this book you should now be in a position to write (or at least begin to write) most of the programs you need, however an introductory book of this nature can not hope to cover all aspects of a language. This chapter is therefore intended to give you some insight into some of the areas which we think are more advanced but of which you should be aware. You should also note that although CA-Clipper is very versatile its power can be increased by the use of many third party libraries which enable you as a programmer to write communication programs, and word processors, access data files created by other systems (including those on mini and mainframe computers), display graphics and do much more.

Pre-processor

Some of you may already be familiar with the idea of a pre-processor, but for those of you who are not, when a program is compiled using CA-Clipper, the first action performed by the compiler is to pass the program through the pre-processor. The pre-processor is a program which takes your source files and converts them into files which the compiler can understand. As has already been suggested, in version 5 there are no longer any commands, these have all been replaced by one or more functions, many of which can also be called by your programs. The action of replacing the commands with the relevant functions is performed by the pre-processor. For a detailed list of which commands are replaced by which combinations of functions look in `STD.CH` which can be found in the directory pointed to by the include environment variable (`\clipper5\include` on a standard configuration). This file contains all the default pre-processor directives used by the compiler. While most of the directives are beyond the scope of this book there are two of which you should be aware, these are **include** and **define**. Pre-processor directives are often used in more than one program, because of this they are usually placed in a separate file and then included at compile time.

```
#include "myfile.ch"
```

will include a copy of `"myfile.ch"` in the current file when it is compiled. There are two points to note about the above directive, these are that include, as with all pre-processor directives is prefixed by a hash sign `(#)` and that it is a convention that all CA-Clipper include files have a '`CH`' extension. CA-Clipper provides several pre-defined include files, these are as follows.

Achoice	***Constants used in achoice()***
Box	Box drawing constants
Dbedit	Constants used by dbedit()
Dbstruct	Constants used by dbstruct()
Directory	Constants used by directory()
Error	Constants used by the error system
Fileio	Constants used in the file handling functions
Getexit	Constants used by the get system
Inkey	Constants for the values returned by inkey()
Memoedit	Constants used by memoedit()
Set	Constants used set()
Setcursor	Constants used by setcursor()
Std	Definitions of standard commands

The second directive that we shall cover is **define**. This can be used to define **manifest constants** and **pseudo-functions**. Manifest constants are used to give names to values, and then when the program is compiled the name is replaced by this value.

```
#define K_ESC 27
```

This will define the constant `K_ESC` as having the value `27` (which is the ASCII value of the escape key). Once defined in this way any reference to the value `27` can be replaced with a reference to the constant `K_ESC`. It should be noted that although it looks like a variable, in reality it does not exist as one and can not therefore be assigned a value. Pseudo-functions are used to replace an identifier with a piece of code which can accept parameters

```
#define MAX(a, b) (if(a > b, a, b))
? MAX(5, 10)
```

If the above piece of code were to be compiled the code passed from the pre-processor to the compiler would be

```
? (if(5 > 10, 5, 10))
```

which would display the value `10`. The difference between a manifest constant and a pseudo-function is that immediately following the identifier for the function must come a parenthesised parameter list. The define directive is case sensitive and because of this it is usual for all identifiers which are to be re-defined to be in upper case.

Code blocks

As this is an introductory book there are many functions which we have not covered, and similarly of those we have chosen there are often parameters which we have for the sake of clarity omitted. In many cases it is possible to pass code blocks to the standard functions in order to modify their behaviour, and so if a function doesn't behave quite as you need you should check the manual to see if it can be modified. We have already seen that

```
INDEX ON cName TO file1
```

will index the field `"name"` in the current file and save the index in a file called FILE1.NTX. When this command is passed to the pre-processor it is converted into the following function call

```
DBCreateIndex("file1","cName",{||cName},if(.f.,.t.,nil))
```

As you can see the first parameter is the name of the file to be created, the second is a string containing the indexing expression (this is written at the beginning of the file and is used when the index is updated). The fourth is a logical value stating whether the index is unique. The third parameter is a code block which is used to index the file. It is called once for each record indexed, and providing its last expression matches the second parameter it can do anything you wish from merely counting the number of records in the index to displaying a bar graph to report the progress of the function. If you were to replace the code block with

```
{||devpos(0,0),qout(recno()),cName}
```

and then call the function it would display the record number at position 0,0 as each record is indexed.

Functions (and when to use them)

We have already seen that all procedures can be replaced by functions but you may still be unsure which pieces of code should be placed in separate functions. As a general rule any piece of code which is used in more than one place should be placed in a function. This is fine as far as it goes, however with the inclusion of code blocks and classes this can be taken further. We have already seen that functions which perform similar (but significantly different) actions can be combined by the use of code blocks, now we shall consider classes. We have seen how to create a table using tbrowse, and stated that to control the table you need a case statement which converts the key press into a call to the relevant method. This is fine provided you only have one table in your program, however it is usual to have several performing different tasks. In this case you would have several loops (one for each table) all containing virtually the same code. An alternative to this is facilitated by the fact that each table is held in a variable which, like any other variable, can be passed as a parameter to a function. This function can then contain a case statement which performs calls to the various methods required, and when called from within the controlling loops of two separate tables will apply the method only to the currently active table. This function will not be able to action all the keys pressed within all the various different tables (one table may be used to display data in which case you could allow editing while another may be a menu), because of this the function can only contain calls to the standard methods and should return a logical value to indicate whether or not the key was processed, it is then up to the calling routine to decide whether any other action should be taken.

Macros

In CA-Clipper there are times when you can not be sure how you want your program to behave until run time. One example of this is to use a filter to specify which records are required on a report, the expression used in the filter could be specified by the user and would not therefore be known in advance. One method of achieving this is to use macro expansion, this is when an expression is compiled at run time, executed and then discarded. To expand a macro it should be prefixed by an ampersand (however if it is a compound expression it should first be surrounded by parentheses).

```
cFilter := "cName = " + "Paul"
SET FILTER TO &cFilter
```

and

```
SET FILTER TO &("cName = " + "Paul")
```

would both set a filter on the current file such that only those records with the value "Paul" in the field cName could be seen. Any expression can be macro expanded provided that if any variables are used, they are declared as either publics or privates but the fact that once the result has been used it is discarded makes it very inefficient.

```
cFunc := "MyFunc"
FOR nCounter := 1 TO 10
   DO &cFunc
NEXT
```

will loop 10 times. Each time it will expand cFunc and call the procedure MyFunc, after which it will discard the expanded macro and loop again.

```
cFunc := &("{||MyFunc()}")
FOR nCounter := 1 TO 10
   eval(cFunc)
NEXT
```

will expand the macro to produce a codeblock, the loop is then executed 10 times and each time a call is made to the function MyFunc. As you can see this method only requires one macro expansion and is therefore much faster.

Note

If a macro is required more than once, performance can be increased by saving the results as a codeblock.

Set()

We have already seen how to change colours this is only one of the environment variables which can be modified by using various commands. Another more convenient way to modify these variables is to use the set() function which being a get/set function, as well as altering the values can be used to report on the current settings. This function accepts three parameters of which only the first is required. The first is a numeric value indicating which setting you require. This value may change from release to release and should only be used via one of the manifest constants supplied in the include file SET.CH. The second parameter is the new value you wish the variable to take. If this value is omitted, the function simply returns the current setting without changing it. Some of the settings open files, if one of these is used, then the third parameter is used to indicate whether it is an existing file which should be appended to or not. Below is a list of the constants along with the equivalent command/function (if any).

Note

set() is a get/set function.

Constant	*Value type*	*Command/function*
_SET_EXACT	Logical	SET EXACT
_SET_FIXED	Logical	SET FIXED
_SET_DECIMALS	Numeric	SET DECIMALS
_SET_DATEFORMAT	Character	SET DATE
_SET_EPOCH	Numeric	SET EPOCH
_SET_PATH	Character	SET PATH
_SET_DEFAULT	Character	SET DEFAULT
_SET_EXCLUSIVE	Logical	SET EXCLUSIVE
_SET_SOFTSEEK	Logical	SET SOFTSEEK
_SET_UNIQUE	Logical	SET UNIQUE
_SET_DELETED	Logical	SET DELETED
_SET_CANCEL	Logical	SETCANCEL()
_SET_DEBUG	Logical	ALTD()
_SET_COLOR	Character	SETCOLOR()
_SET_CURSOR	Numeric	SETCURSOR()
_SET_CONSOLE	Logical	SET CONSOLE
_SET_ALTERNATE	Logical	SET ALTERNATE
_SET_ALTFILE	Character	SET ALTERNATE TO
_SET_DEVICE	Character	SET DEVICE
_SET_EXTRAFILE	Character	
_SET_PRINTER	Logical	SET PRINTER
_SET_PRINTFILE	Character	SET PRINTER TO
_SET_MARGIN	Numeric	SET MARGIN
_SET_BELL	Logical	SET BELL
_SET_CONFIRM	Logical	SET CONFIRM
_SET_ESCAPE	Logical	SET ESCAPE
_SET_INSERT	Logical	READINSERT()
_SET_EXIT	Logical	READEXIT()
_SET_INTENSITY	Logical	SET INTENSITY
_SET_SCOREBOARD	Logical	SET SCOREBOARD
_SET_DELIMITERS	Logical	SET DELIMITERS
_SET_DELIMCHARS	Character	SET DELIMITERS TO
_SET_WRAP	Logical	SET WRAP
_SET_MESSAGE	Numeric	SET MESSAGE
_SET_MCENTER	Logical	SET MESSAGE
_SET_SCROLLBREAK	Logical	

SET.CH also defines the constant _SET_COUNT to be the number of values accessible by set(). This constant can be used to control loops which save and restore all the set values in the following manner.

```
#include "set.ch"

FUNCTION aSaveSet()

    LOCAL aSets := {}, nCount
    FOR nCount := 1 TO _SET_COUNT
       aadd(aSets,set(nCount))
    NEXT
RETURN aSets
```

Summary

In this chapter we have seen how to use the pre-processor to define manifest constants and pseudo-functions. We have seen how codeblocks can be used to add functionality to existing functions and how to use the get/set function set() to configure the environment variables. We have also seen how to use macros to compile sections of code at run time and mentioned how these can be saved in codeblocks.

Problems

8.1 *Write the function to restore the* set() *values which were saved by the function* aSaveSet().

8.2 *Write the function mentioned above which can be used to control a* tbrowse.

9 Solutions

Problem 1.1

```
/*Display the numbers since the start of the day save in
the file seconds.prg*/

FUNCTION Seconds()

    LOCAL nHours, nMinutes, nSeconds
    CLEAR SCREEN
    nHours   := 0
    nMinutes := 0
    @ 0,0  SAY "Hour   :"
    @ 1,0  SAY "Minute :"
    @ 0,10 GET nHours
    @ 1,10 GET nMinutes
    READ
    nSeconds := ((nHours * 60) + nMinutes) * 60
    @ 2,0  SAY "The number of seconds is"
    @ 2,25 SAY nSeconds
RETURN nil
```

Problem 2.1

```
/*Display the larger of two numbers*/

FUNCTION Larger()

    LOCAL nNumber1, nNumber2, nLargest
    CLEAR SCREEN
    nNumber1 := 0
    nNumber2 := 0
    @ 0,0  SAY "First  :"
    @ 1,0  SAY "Second :"
    @ 0,10 GET nNumber1
    @ 1,10 GET nNumber2
    READ
    nLargest := max(nNumber1, nNumber2)
    @ 2,0  SAY "The larger is"
    @ 2,14 SAY nLargest
RETURN nil
```

Problem 2.2

```
/*Concatenates two strings*/

FUNCTION Message()

    LOCAL cName, cMessage
    CLEAR SCREEN
    cName := "          "
    @ 0,0 SAY "Name :"
    @ 0,7 GET cName
    READ
    cMessage := "Welcome " + cName
    @ 1,0 SAY cMessage
RETURN nil
```

Problem 2.3

```
/*Displays the date with the month name*/

FUNCTION Showdate()

  LOCAL dDate, cDateString
  CLEAR SCREEN
  dDate := date()
  cDateString := str(day(dDate)) + ", " + cmonth(dDate) ;
                    + str(year(dDate))
    @ 1,0 SAY cDateString
RETURN nil
```

Problem 3.1

```
/*Displays a box returning the screen beneath it*/

FUNCTION cBox(nTop, nLeft, nBottom, nRight, cString)

    LOCAL cScreen
    cScreen := savescreen(nTop, nLeft, nBottom, nRight)
    dispbox(nTop, nLeft, nBottom, nRight, cString)
RETURN cScreen
```

Problem 3.2

```
/*Scrolling get*/

FUNCTION Get()

    LOCAL cString
    CLS
    cString := "                    "
    dispbox(0,0,2,11,"╓─╖║╜─╙║ ")
    @ 1,1 GET cString PICTURE "@s10"
    READ
    @ 3,0 SAY "The string entered was - " + cString
RETURN nil
```

Problem 3.3

```
/*Memoedit function*/

FUNCTION Memo()

    CLS
    dispbox(0,0,20,20,"╓─╖║╜─╙║ ")
    memoedit(,1,1,19,19,.t.,"nPos")
RETURN nil

FUNCTION nPos(nMode, nRow, nCol)

    @ 21,0  SAY "Row :    Col :"
    @ 21,6  SAY nRow PICTURE "99"
    @ 21,15 SAY nCol PICTURE "99"
RETURN 0
```

Problem 4.1

```
/*This function can be replaced by the CA-Clipper
function replicate() or when the character is a space the
function space()*/

FUNCTION cRepeat(nNumber, cChar)

    LOCAL nCounter, cRet
    cRet := ""
    FOR nCounter := 1 TO nNumber
```

```
        cRet := cRet + cChar
    NEXT
RETURN cRet
```

Problem 4.2

```
/*Accepts grades and reports on the spread*/

FUNCTION Bands()

    LOCAL aBands, nGrade
    CLS
    aBands := {0,0,0,0,0,0}
    nGrade := 0
    @ 0,0  SAY "Enter the first grade (or -1 to exit)"
    @ 0,38 GET nGrade PICTURE "999" VALID (nGrade <= 100)
    READ
    DO WHILE nGrade > -1
       DO CASE
          CASE nGrade > 84
               aBands[1] := aBands[1] + 1
          CASE nGrade > 69
               aBands[2] := aBands[2] + 1
          CASE nGrade > 54
               aBands[3] := aBands[3] + 1
          CASE nGrade > 39
               aBands[4] := aBands[4] + 1
          CASE nGrade > 29
               aBands[5] := aBands[5] + 1
          OTHERWISE
              aBands[6] := aBands[6] + 1
      ENDCASE
     nGrade := 0
     @ 0,0  SAY "Enter the next grade (or -1 to exit) "
     @ 0,37 GET nGrade PICTURE "999" VALID (nGrade <= 100)
     READ
    ENDDO
    @ 2,0  SAY "There were     grades in band A"
    @ 3,0  SAY "There were     grades in band B"
    @ 4,0  SAY "There were     grades in band C"
    @ 5,0  SAY "There were     grades in band D"
    @ 6,0  SAY "There were     grades in band E"
    @ 7,0  SAY "There were     grades in band U"
    @ 2,10 SAY aBands[1] PICTURE "9999"
    @ 3,10 SAY aBands[2] PICTURE "9999"
```

```
    @ 4,10 SAY aBands[3] PICTURE "9999"
    @ 5,10 SAY aBands[4] PICTURE "9999"
    @ 6,10 SAY aBands[5] PICTURE "9999"
    @ 7,10 SAY aBands[6] PICTURE "9999"
RETURN nil
```

Problem 4.3

```
/*Shows the first 20 numbers in the Fibonacci sequence*/

FUNCTION Fib()

    LOCAL nFirst, nSecond, nNext, nCount
    CLS
    nFirst  := 1
    nSecond := 1
    nNext   := 1
    ? nFirst
    ? nSecond
    FOR nCount  := 1 TO 18
        nFirst  := nSecond
        nSecond := nNext
        nNext   := nFirst + nSecond
        ? nNext
    NEXT
RETURN nil
```

Problem 4.4

```
/*Takes four arrays and an initial option number as input
parameters.To make this function more secure the type and
length of the parameters should be checked to ensure that
they are all of the correct types and sizes.In doing this
you could also allow for either (but not both the row or
column arrays to be replaced with a single value.*/

FUNCTION nMenu(aRow, aCol, aPrompt, aMessage, nOption)

    LOCAL nCount
    FOR nCount := 1 TO LEN(aRow)
        @ aRow[nCount], aCol[nCount] ;
          PROMPT aPrompt[nCount] MESSAGE aMessage[nCount]
    NEXT
    MENU TO nOption
RETURN nOption
```

Problem 5.1

```
/*Adds records to customer.dbf*/

FUNCTION Addrec()

    LOCAL cName, cAdd1, cAdd2
    LOCAL cPost, cTel, nInvoice
    USE customer
    DO WHILE lastkey() != 27
        CLS
        cName    := space(30)
        cAdd1    := space(50)
        cAdd2    := space(50)
        cPost    := space(8)
        cTel     := space(15)
        nInvoice := 0
        @ 0,0  SAY "Name           :" GET cName
        @ 1,0  SAY "Address        :" GET cAdd1
        @ 2,17 GET cAdd2
        @ 3,0  SAY "Post code      :" GET cPost
        @ 3,26 SAY "Tel :" GET cTel
        @ 4,0  SAY "Invoice Number :" GET nInvoice
        READ
        IF lastkey() != 27
            APPEND BLANK
            customer->cName    := cName
            customer->cAdd1    := cAdd1
            customer->cAdd2    := cAdd2
            customer->cPost    := cPost
            customer->cTel     := cTel
            customer->nInvoice := nInvoice
        ENDIF
    ENDDO
RETURN nil
```

Problem 5.2

```
/*Searches customer.dbf for certain records.
 (uses cBox() from problem 3.1)*/

FUNCTION Search()

    LOCAL cName, cScreen
    USE customer INDEX name
```

```
    DO WHILE lastkey() != 27
        CLS
        cName := space(30)
        @ 0,0  SAY "Name           :" GET cName
        @ 1,0  SAY "Address        :"
        @ 3,0  SAY "Post code      :"
        @ 3,26 SAY "Tel :"
        @ 4,0  SAY "Invoice Number :"
        READ
        IF lastkey() != 27
            SEEK cName
            IF found()
              @ 1,17 SAY customer->cAdd1
              @ 2,17 SAY customer->cAdd2
              @ 3,17 SAY customer->cPost
              @ 3,32 SAY customer->cTel
              @ 4,17 SAY customer->nInvoice
              inkey(0)
            ELSE
               cScreen := cBox(2,10,4,27,"╓─╖║╜─╙║ ")
               @ 3,11 SAY "No Record Found!"
               inkey(0)
               restscreen(2,10,4,27,screen)
            ENDIF
        ENDIF
    ENDDO
RETURN nil
```

Problem 5.3

```
/*Displays the contents of c:\autoexec.bat*/

FUNCTION Autoexec()

    Local nHandle, cBuffer, lEof, nPos
    nPos    := 0
    lEof    := .f.
    cBuffer := space(255)
    IF (nHandle := fopen("c:\autoexec.bat")) >= 0
        DO WHILE ! lEof
            IF fread(nHandle, @cBuffer, 255) = 0
                lEof := .t.
                /*the end of the file has been found*/
            ELSE
                ? left(cBuffer,at(chr(13), cBuffer))
```

```
                nPos := nPos + at(chr(13), cBuffer) + 1
                fseek(nHandle, nPos)
            ENDIF
        ENDDO
    ELSE
        ? "The file could not be opened"
    ENDIF
RETURN nil
```

Problem 6.1

```
Subtract := {|nFirst, nSecond|nFirst - nSecond}
Divide := {|nFirst, nSecond|nFirst / nSecond}
```

Problem 6.2

```
/*Achoice() list of names*/
FUNCTION Names()

    LOCAL nRecord
    PRIVATE aNames
    /*must be private to be in scope in control()*/
    CLS
    aNames := {"Paul"}
    dispbox(0,0,10,27,"╓╥╖║╜─╙║ ")
    nRecord := 0
    DO WHILE lastkey() != 27 .AND. nRecord = 0
      nRecord := achoice(1,1,9,26,aNames,.t.,"nControl")
    ENDDO
    IF lastkey() = 27
      @ 12,0 SAY "Selection was aborted"
    ELSE
      @ 12,0 SAY rtrim(aNames[nRecord]) + " was selected"
    ENDIF
RETURN nil

FUNCTION nControl(nMode, nElement, nRow)

    LOCAL cScreen, cName, nRet, nKey
    nKey := lastkey()
    nRet := 2
    IF nMode = 3
        DO CASE
          CASE upper(chr(nKey)) = "A"
            cScreen := cBox(2,0,4,27,"╓╥╖║╜─╙║ ")
```

```
            cName    := space(25)
            @ 3,1 GET cName
            READ
            restscreen(2,0,4,27,cScreen)
            IF lastkey() != 27
              aadd(cNames,cName)
              nRet := 0
            ENDIF
          CASE nKey = 27
            nRet := 0
          CASE nKey = 13
            nRet := 1
        ENDCASE
    ENDIF
RETURN nRet
```

Problem 6.3

```
/*This merely uses a combination of the examples given in
the text.  The table is in invoice number order.*/

FUNCTION Table()

    LOCAL oBrowse, nKey
    USE customer INDEX invoice
    USE invoice NEW
    SET RELATION TO nNumber INTO customer
    CLS
    oBrowse := TBrowseDB(1,1,20,60)
    oBrowse:addColumn( ;
        TBColumnNew("Name",{||customer->cName}))
    oBrowse:addColumn( ;
        TBColumnNew("Add1",{||customer->cAdd1}))
    oBrowse:addColumn( ;
        TBColumnNew("Add2",{||customer->cAdd2}))
    oBrowse:addColumn( ;
        TBColumnNew("Post",{||customer->cPost}))
    oBrowse:addColumn( ;
        TBColumnNew("Tel",{||customer->cTel}))
    oBrowse:addColumn( ;
        TBColumnNew("Invoice",{||customer->nInvoice}))
    oBrowse:addColumn( ;
        TBColumnNew("Number",{||invoice->nNumber}))
    key := 0
    DO WHILE key != 27
```

```
        DO WHILE !oBrowse:Stabilize()
        ENDDO
        nKey := inkey(0)
        DO CASE
            CASE nKey == 5
                oBrowse:up()
            CASE nKey == 24
                oBrowse:down()
            CASE nKey == 4
                oBrowse:right()
            CASE nKey == 19
                oBrowse:left()
        ENDCASE
    ENDDO
RETURN nil
```

Problem 6.4

```
/*This function will browse any array passed to it using
a column width equal to the length of the first element
in the array.  It uses two functions max() and min()
which return the maximum and minimum of the two numbers
passed to them respectively.*/

FUNCTION browse(aArray)

  LOCAL nRecPointer := 1, oTable, nKey, oColumn
  @ 0, 0 to 24, 79
  oTable := TBrowseNew(1, 1, 23, 78)
  oTable:goTopBlock    := {||nRecPointer := 1}
  oTable:goBottomBlock := {||nRecPointer := len(aArray)}
  oTable:skipBlock := {|nRec, nOld| nOld := nRecPointer,;
      nRecPointer := if(nRec > 0, min(len(aArray),;
      nRecPointer + nRec), max(1, nRecPointer + nRec)),;
      nRecPointer - nOld}
  oColumn := TBColumnNew(,{||aArray[nRecPointer]})
  oTable:addColumn(oColumn)
  nKey := 0
  DO WHILE nKey != 27
        DO WHILE !oTable:Stabilize()
        ENDDO
        nKey := inkey(0)
        DO CASE
            CASE nKey == 5
                oTable:up()
```

```
            CASE nKey == 24
                oTable:down()
            CASE nKey == 4
                oTable:right()
            CASE nKey == 19
                oTable:left()
        ENDCASE
    ENDDO
RETURN nil
```

Problem 7.1

```
/*When included in your programs this will enable
you to edit and save help screens in the file HELP.DBF*/

FUNCTION Help(cName, nLine, cVar)

    LOCAL nArea := select()
    LOCAL cScreen, nTopRow, nTopCol, nBotRow, nBotCol
    LOCAL lFound, cText, nOption, getlist := {}
    nTopRow := nTopCol := nBotRow := nBotCol := 0
    USE help INDEX help NEW
    IF (lFound := dbseek (left(cName + space(10), 10) + ;
       str(nLine, 10) + left(cVar + space(10), 10)))
        nTopRow := toprow
        nTopCol := topcol
        nBotRow := botrow
        nBotCol := botcol
        cText   := text
    ENDIF
    nOption := 1
    DO WHILE lastkey() != 27
        cScreen := savescreen(0, 0, 4, 13)
        dispbox(0, 0, 4, 13, "╔═╗║╝═╚║ ")
        @ 1, 1 PROMPT "Co-ordinates"
        @ 2, 1 PROMPT "Edit text"
        @ 3, 1 PROMPT "Save text"
        MENU TO nOption
        restscreen(0, 0, 4, 13, cScreen)
        DO CASE
            CASE nOption == 1
                cScreen := savescreen(0, 0, 3, 23)
                dispbox(0, 0, 3, 23, "╔═╗║╝═╚║ ")
                @ 1, 1 SAY "Top    row    col"
                @ 2, 1 SAY "Bottom row    col"
```

```
                @ 1, 12 GET nTopRow picture "99"
                @ 1, 19 GET nTopCol picture "99"
                @ 2, 12 GET nBotRow picture "99"
                @ 2, 19 GET nBotCol picture "99"
                READ
                restscreen(0, 0, 3, 23, cScreen)
            CASE nOption == 2 .and. (nBotRow - nTopRow > ;
               1) .and. (nBotCol - nTopCol > 1)
               cScreen := savescreen(nTopRow, nTopCol, ;
                   nBotRow, nBotCol)
               dispbox(nTopRow, nTopCol, nBotRow, nBotCol;
                     , "╔═╗║╝═╚║ ")
               cText := memoedit(cText, nTopRow + 1, ;
                   nTopCol + 1, nBotRow - 1, nBotCol - 1)
               restscreen(nTopRow, nTopCol, nBotRow, ;
                   nBotCol, cScreen)
            CASE nOption == 3
                IF ! lFound
                    APPEND BLANK
                    lFound := .t.
                ENDIF
                help->name    := cName
                help->line    := nLine
                help->var     := cVar
                help->toprow  := nTopRow
                help->topcol  := nTopCol
                help->botrow  := nBotRow
                help->botcol  := nBotCol
                help->text    := cText
        ENDCASE
    ENDDO
    CLOSE
    select(nArea)
RETURN nil
```

Problem 7.2

```
/*The desired results can be achieved by simply adding
the following to the case statement in the DateReader()
function in the chapter.*/

CASE nKey == 31
    dDate := oGet:unTransform()
    if month(dDate) = 12
        ddate := ctod(left(dtoc(dDate), 3) + "01/" + ;
```

```
            str(year(dDate) + 1))
    else
         ddate := ctod(left(dtoc(dDate), 3) + ;
           str(month(dDate) + 1) + substr(dtoc(dDate), 6))
    endif
    oGet:buffer := transform(dDate, oGet:picture)
CASE nKey == 30
    dDate := oGet:unTransform()
    if month(dDate) = 1
         ddate := ctod(left(dtoc(dDate), 3) + "12/" + ;
           str(year(dDate) - 1))
    else
         ddate := ctod(left(dtoc(dDate), 3) + ;
           str(month(dDate) - 1) + substr(dtoc(dDate), 6))
    endif
    oGet:buffer := transform(dDate, oGet:picture)
CASE nKey == 409
    dDate := oGet:unTransform()
    dDate := ctod(left(dtoc(dDate), 6) + str(year(dDate) ;
              + 1))
    oGet:buffer := transform(dDate, oGet:picture)
CASE nKey == 417
    dDate := oGet:unTransform()
    dDate := ctod(left(dtoc(dDate), 6) + str(year(dDate) ;
              - 1))
    oGet:buffer := transform(dDate, oGet:picture)
```

Problem 8.1

```
FUNCTION RestSets(aSets)

    LOCAL nCount
    FOR nCount := 1 TO _SET_COUNT
        set(nCount,aSets[nCount])
    NEXT
RETURN nil
```

Problem 8.2

```
/*When passed the table and the ascii code of the key
pressed control will action the key if appropriate
returning a logical indicating success/failure.
It uses the header file INKEY.CH*/

FUNCTION lControl(oBrowse, nKey)
```

```
    LOCAL lRet := .t.
    DO CASE
       CASE nKey == K_HOME
            oBrowse:home()
       CASE nKey == K_CTRL_RIGHT
            oBrowse:panRight()
       CASE nKey == K_PGDN
            oBrowse:pageDown()
       CASE nKey == K_RIGHT
            oBrowse:right()
       CASE nKey == K_UP
            oBrowse:up()
       CASE nKey == K_END
            oBrowse:end()
       CASE nKey == K_PGUP
            oBrowse:pageUp()
       CASE nKey == K_LEFT
            oBrowse:left()
       CASE nKey == K_CTRL_END
            oBrowse:panEnd()
       CASE nKey == K_DOWN
            oBrowse:down()
       CASE nKey == K_CTRL_LEFT
            oBrowse:panLeft()
       CASE nKey == K_CTRL_HOME
            oBrowse:panHome()
       CASE nKey == K_CTRL_PGDN
            oBrowse:goBottom()
       CASE nKey == K_CTRL_PGUP
            oBrowse:goTop()
       OTHERWISE
            lRet := .f.
    ENDCASE
RETURN lRet
```

A Inkey codes

Below is a table of the key codes as returned by the inkey() function.

Cursor movement keys

Key	*Value*	*Manifest constant*
Uparrow	5	K_UP
Dnarrow	24	K_DOWN
Leftarrow	19	K_LEFT
Rightarrow	4	K_RIGHT
Home	1	K_HOME
End	6	K_END
PgUp	18	K_PGUP
PgDn	3	K_PGDN
Ctrl-Leftarrow	26	K_CTRL_LEFT
Ctrl-Rightarrow	2	K_CTRL_RIGHT
Ctrl-Home	29	K_CTRL_HOME
Ctrl-End	23	K_CTRL_END
Ctrl-PgUp	31	K_CTRL_PGUP
Ctrl-PgDn	30	K_CTRL_PGDN
Ctrl-Return	10	K_CTRL_RET
Ctrl-Scroll Lock	3	K_CTRL_C
Esc	27	K_ESC
Return	13	K_RETURN
Enter	13	K_ENTER

Editing keys

Key	*Value*	*Manifest constant*
Del	7	K_DEL
Tab	9	K_TAB
Shift-Tab	271	K_SH_TAB
Ins	22	K_INS
Backspace	8	K_BS
Ctrl-Backspace	127	K_CTRL_BS

Function keys

Key	*Value*	*Manifest constant*
F1	28	K_F1
F2	-1	K_F2

Key	*Value*	*Manifest constant*
F3	-2	K_F3
F4	-3	K_F4
F5	-4	K_F5
F6	-5	K_F6
F7	-6	K_F7
F8	-7	K_F8
F9	-8	K_F9
F10	-9	K_F10

Shift, Alt, and Ctrl-function keys

Key	*Value*	*Manifest constant*
Shift-F1	-10	K_SH_F1
Shift-F2	-11	K_SH_F2
Shift-F3	-12	K_SH_F3
Ctrl-F1	-20	K_CTRL_F1
Ctrl-F2	-21	K_CTRL_F2
Ctrl-F3	-22	K_CTRL_F3
Alt-F1	-30	K_ALT_F1
Alt-F2	-31	K_ALT_F2
Alt-F3	-32	K_ALT_F3

Alt and Ctrl keys

Key	*Value*	*Manifest constant*
Alt-A	286	K_ALT_A
Alt-B	304	K_ALT_B
Alt-C	302	K_ALT_C
Alt-D	288	K_ALT_D
Alt-E	274	K_ALT_E
Alt-F	289	K_ALT_F
Alt-G	290	K_ALT_G
Alt-H	291	K_ALT_H
Alt-I	279	K_ALT_I
Alt-J	292	K_ALT_J
Alt-K	293	K_ALT_K
Alt-L	294	K_ALT_L
Alt-M	306	K_ALT_M
Alt-N	305	K_ALT_N
Alt-O	280	K_ALT_O
Alt-P	281	K_ALT_P

Key	***Value***	***Manifest constant***
Alt-Q	272	K_ALT_Q
Alt-R	275	K_ALT_R
Alt-S	287	K_ALT_S
Alt-T	276	K_ALT_T
Alt-U	278	K_ALT_U
Alt-V	303	K_ALT_V
Alt-W	273	K_ALT_W
Alt-X	301	K_ALT_X
Alt-Y	277	K_ALT_Y
Alt-Z	300	K_ALT_Z
Ctrl-A	1	K_CTRL_A
Ctrl-B	2	K_CTRL_B
Ctrl-C	3	K_CTRL_C
Ctrl-D	4	K_CTRL_D
Ctrl-E	5	K_CTRL_E
Ctrl-F	6	K_CTRL_F
Ctrl-G	7	K_CTRL_G
Ctrl-H	8	K_CTRL_H
Ctrl-I	9	K_CTRL_I
Ctrl-J	10	K_CTRL_J
Ctrl-K	11	K_CTRL_K
Ctrl-L	12	K_CTRL_L
Ctrl-M	13	K_CTRL_M
Ctrl-N	14	K_CTRL_N
Ctrl-O	15	K_CTRL_O
Ctrl-P	16	K_CTRL_P
Ctrl-Q	17	K_CTRL_Q
Ctrl-R	18	K_CTRL_R
Ctrl-S	19	K_CTRL_S
Ctrl-T	20	K_CTRL_T
Ctrl-U	21	K_CTRL_U
Ctrl-V	22	K_CTRL_V
Ctrl-W	23	K_CTRL_W
Ctrl-X	24	K_CTRL_X
Ctrl-Y	25	K_CTRL_Y
Ctrl-Z	26	K_CTRL_Z

B Compiling, linking and making

This appendix covers the use of the compiler, and linker which together convert your programs into the executable files that can run on your computer. It also covers the make facility supplied with CA-Clipper. It is not a detailed discussion but should provide you with sufficient knowledge to compile most systems.

Compiling

Compiling is the process of converting your source files into object files, and as such the most important (and indeed the only mandatory) parameter to pass to the compiler is the name of the source file. The filename may include the path and if an extension other than .PRG has been used then this should also be included. The default behaviour of the compiler is to create an object file with the extension of .OBJ containing a compiled version of your program, it will also create an initial function with the same name as the program file, and include any .PRG's which are referenced by a do command (i.e. are called as procedures). This behaviour can be modified in two ways, the first is the use of a script file which lists the .PRG's to be included in the .obj and prevents the compiler from searching for any more, the second is the use of compiler option switches which can either be added as further parameters (prefixed with a forward slash) or held in the CLIPPERCMD environment variable. If a script file is to be used it should replace the source filename as the input parameter to the compiler and to distinguish it from a source file should be prefixed with an at sign ('@'). Below is a list of some of the compiler switches.

B	Include the information required for the debugger to work.
L	Don't include line numbers in the object. (makes smaller object files but hinders debugging.)
M	Compile only the current source file. (the same as including it in a scrip file.)
N	Suppress the creation of the main procedure.
O	Specify a different name for the object file.
P	Produce a file containing the output from the pre-processor. This file has the same name as the source file but an extension of .PPO.
R	Include a reference to a library. (used for linking.)
S	Check the syntax of the source files but don't produce an object file.
Z	Prevent the shortcutting of logical operators. (see chapter 4.)

```
clipper average /n
```

will therefore compile the program average.prg seen in chapter 1.

Linking

The compiler produces an object file with the same name as the program file but with an extension of OBJ. This file must now be linked with various library files in order that an executable file can be generated. The linker provided with CA-Clipper is RTLink and can receive its parameters in one of three ways. The first way to pass these parameters is FREEFORMAT which is where the different types of parameters are prefixed with keywords and is of greatest use when using script files. The second is POSITIONAL in which the parameter types are separated by commas and being shorter than the freeformat method is better suited to use on the MS-DOS command line. The third method really applies to both of the previous ones in that if RTLink requires a parameter which has been omitted it will enter an interactive mode and prompt you for the missing parameters. There are three keywords in the freeformat mode these are file, output, and library, whereas the positional mode requires the parameters in the following order, the list of object files, the name of the output file, the name of the map file (used to report the addresses of the routines), a list of library files, and any switches. The switches can be placed in the environment variable RTLINKCMD, on the command line or in a script file but only come into effect when the input switches from one stream to another (i.e. a switch placed on the command line only affects parameters placed in a script file). When the linker runs it places all routines found in the object file list into the output file, it then tries to resolve any remaining references to functions by searching the library files from which it only copies those functions required therefore, if you require all the functions in a library to be included in an EXE file but do not call the functions explicitly simply include the library name in the list of object files. If you intend to write several applications which use the same libraries it is possible to create a pre-link library which contains the functions to be used. Your applications can then use this library without having to have it linked-in, in this way you can reduce the amount of time it takes to link your applications. Another method of reducing the time it takes to link an application is to use incremental linking, this is where the linker only replaces those .OBJ files which have changed since the last time it was linked. A list of some of the switches is below

Switch	***Description***
BATCH	Prevent interactive mode.
FREEFORMAT	Select freeformat parameter input.
POSITIONAL	Select positional parameter input.

Switch	***Description***
INCREMENTAL	Select incremental linking.
PLL	Specify the prelink library to be used with this EXE.
PRELINK	Create a prelink library instead of an EXE file.

Note

If all the functions within a library are to be included in the .EXE it should be listed along with the .OBJs. However you must remember to include its extension.

There are two main advantages to using scrip files, the first is the way large lists of files and libraries can be included and the other is the ability to define overlays. Overlays are sections of code which use the same area of memory and can therefore be used to run programs which are larger than the available memory. There are two types of overlays, dynamic and static. All CA-Clipper code linked using RTLink is dynamically overlaid meaning that unused code is replaced by new code as it is needed. The old code is replaced on a least used basis. Any code written in a language other than CA-Clipper can only be overlaid using static overlays, the object file to be placed in an overlay should be prefixed with the keyword SECTION, the overlays which are to use the same area in memory should be grouped together and surrounded with the keywords BEGINAREA and ENDAREA.

Making

While working on a system involving more than one object file it is unlikely that you will need to recompile all the files, however it is not always easy to remember which files have been changed. To overcome this problem CA-Clipper provides the utility RMAKE which compares each .OBJ or .EXE with it's constituent files to determine which ones need to be updated and then takes whatever actions are defined to update these files. The way RMAKE works is very simple the destination file is followed by a list of the files which go to make it (the destination and constituent files are separated by a colon). If any of the constituent files have a later time or date stamp RMAKE will perform the actions listed on the lines following the files, this list of actions must be indented by a space or tab character and is terminated by a blank line.

```
test1.obj: test1.prg
    clipper test1 /n

test2.obj: test2.prg
    clipper test2 /n

test.exe: test1.obj, test2.obj
    rtlink @test
```

The RMAKE script file shown above will first compare each object file with it's source file and if the source file has been updated since it was last compiled it is then recompiled. Having done this the executable file is compared with the objects to decide whether or not to relink and if the link script stated that incremental linking was to be used only those objects which had changed would be replaced. By using RMAKE in conjunction with incremental linking you can see that the time taken to recompile and link a system can be dramatically reduced.

C The CA-Clipper debugger

This appendix covers the source code debugger supplied with CA-Clipper. In order that it can be used to debug a program, that program must first be compiled using the /b option. The debugger must then be made available to the program at run time, this can be done in one of two ways, the first is to pass the program name along with any parameters required as parameters to CLD (the debugger). This enables you to also pass to the debugger it's own parameters which are the number of lines to be displayed (/43 or /50) or /s which tells the debugger to use the upper half of the screen (in 43 or 50 line mode) to display the program output and the lower half of the screen for the debugger output, and the name of a script file (preceded by an at sign) containing any commands which can be typed in the command window (see later). The second way to provide the debugger is to include the CLD.LIB file as one of the object files when the program is linked.

Note

Including the debugger at link time uses less memory but prevents the initial use of script files and the use of such commands as restart.

This appendix is divided into two sections the first being a description of the various windows available along with their uses and the second a list of the commands.

Windows

There are two types of windows in the CA-Clipper debugger, the first being those which once opened can remain open whilst processing continues, and the second those which must be closed before any other activities may be commenced. The persistent windows can be switched between using the tab and shift tab keys, their order is Code, Monitor, Watch, Callstack, and Command with the currently active window having a double lined edge.

Callstack This window lists the names of the functions and procedures which are currently being processed in the order in which they were called with the active one at the top.

Code This window contains the source code being viewed, it may also contain the output from the pre-processor if required. As the program is executed the current line is highlighted. If the cursor is moved while this window is inactive the results will not be shown until the next time this window is selected.

Colors This window enables you to change the colours used by the debugger.

Command This is the window into which commands are typed, and in which results are displayed. It does not however need to be active for commands to be issued.

Help This window gives a list of subjects down the left with detailed help on each subject in the rest of the window. The subjects can be changed using the up and down arrow keys while the text can be scrolled using the page up and page down keys.

Monitor This window is used to view the contents of any variables being monitored. The values displayed are those pertaining to the routine currently selected from the callstack and are not therefore necessarily the current values of the variables.

Sets This option allows you to view and alter the current values held for each of the set commands.

Watch This window lists any watchpoints or tracepoints which have been defined along with their values. A watchpoint is an expression whose value is to be monitored. A tracepoint is the same as a watchpoint except that if its value changes while the program is being animated execution will halt and control will be returned to the debugger.

Workareas This option lists the currently open data files down the left. On the right of the window is the structure of the file currently selected from the list (not necessarily the currently selected file). In the middle of the window is information pertaining to the status of the file including the record number, the field values for the current record, which indexes are open and which relations are set. The information in this part of the window can be expanded or contracted by highlighting the option and pressing the return key.

Commands

With a few exceptions all the commands have an equivalent menu option and indeed most of the commands contain the menu name as part of their name. Below is a list of the commands grouped by menu, to issue a command you should prefix it with the name of its menu (this can be abbreviated to the first letter) and follow it with any parameters required. If the parameters are not included you will be prompted for them. Many of these commands have key combinations which can be used instead, these can be found next to the command on the menu.

File

Open Displays the contents of other files in the code window, if no extension is included .PRG is assumed. Any breakpoints set are retained after the file is closed.

Resume Returns the currently processed file to the code window.

Dos shell Creates a MS-DOS shell enabling you to execute other programs. To return to the debugger type EXIT.

Exit Leave the debugger.

Locate

Find Searches from the top of the file in the code window for the specified string.

Next Repeats the last find from the current position in the file.

Previous Searches up the file from the current position in the file. If no previous search has been performed you will be prompted for the string.

Goto line Moves the cursor to the specified line.

Case sensitive

Switches on (or off) case sensitivity for the above locate commands.

View

Sets	Opens the sets window.
Workareas	Opens the workareas window.
App screen	Displays the program output.
Callstack	Opens the callstack window.

Run

Restart	Restarts the program.
Animate	Executes each line until a tracepoint or breakpoint is encountered.
Step	Executes the currently highlighted line (if the current line is a function or procedure call the function/procedure is entered).
Trace	Executes the currently highlighted line (if the current line is a function or procedure call the function/procedure is executed in one step).
Go	Executes the program until the next breakpoint or tracepoint is encountered.
To cursor	Executes the program until the line on which the cursor is placed is encountered.
Next routine	Executes the program until the next function or procedure is entered.
Speed	Specifies the delay between executing each line in animation mode.

Point

Watchpoint	Creates a watchpoint for the specified expression.
Tracepoint	Creates a tracepoint for the specified expression.
Breakpoint	Creates a breakpoint for the line where the cursor is currently placed.

Delete Deletes the watchpoint or tracepoint on the specified line in the watch window.

Monitor

Public Monitors all public variables.

Private Monitors all private variables declared in the currently selected routine from the callstack window (or current routine if the callstack window is not open).

Static Monitor all static variables which are visible to the currently selected routine.

Local Monitor all local variables declared in the currently selected routine.

All Enables you to select or deselect all the classes of variables to be monitored.

Sort Enables you to sort the monitored variables into alphabetical order or group into classes.

Options

Preprocessed code

Includes the output of the preprocessor in the code window (requires the program to be compiled with the /p option).

Line numbers

Displays line numbers in the code window.

Exchange screens

Prevents the program output being displayed after each line of code is executed.

Swap on input
Prevents the debugger switching to the program display when accepting input.

Codeblock trace
When stepping over a line containing a codeblock the cursor will move to the line on which the codeblock was defined.

Menu bar Removes the menu bar from the top of the screen.

Mono display
Toggles the display between colour and monochrome.

Colors Opens the colors window.

Tab width Defines the number of spaces to replace each tab with.

Path for files Defines the path used to search for files not stored in the current directory.

Save settings Stores the current debugger configuration to a script file.

Restore settings
Executes a script file.

Window

Next Moves to the next window.

Prev Moves to the last window.

Move Repositions the current window.

Size Changes the size of the current window. (only allows the right and bottom edges to be moved.)

Zoom Expands the current window to fill the screen.

Iconize Reduces the current window to an icon containing its name.

Tile	Returns the windows to their original sizes and positions.

Help

About help	Opens the help window and selects the 'about help' subject.
Keys	Opens the help window and selects the 'keys' subject.
Windows	Opens the help window and selects the 'windows' subject.
Menus	Opens the help window and selects the 'menus' subject.
Commands	Opens the help window and selects the 'commands' subject.

The following commands are not available through the menus.

?	Evaluate an expression returning its result. This command can also be used to declare private variables.
??	The same as ? with the exception that the result is displayed in a popup window.
List	Lists any watchpoints, tracepoints and breakpoints which have been defined.
Num	Switches on or off the line numbers in the code window.
Output	Displays the application screen.
Quit	Exits the debugger.
View	Opens a file displaying its contents in the code window. This command is similar to file open but does not assume any extension.

D The programmers editor, report and label writer and database utility

CA-Clipper is supplied with three utilities which can be used to assist you in the development of your systems: these are the programmers editor, the report and label writer, and the database utility.

The programmers editor

In chapter one we stated that CA-Clipper source programs are stored in text files which can be edited by any program which is capable of creating such files. However as most modern word processors are inappropriate for such a task and text editors are not the most common of programs, CA-Clipper is supplied with an editor of its own called PE. This editor can be found along with the rest of CA-Clippers utilities in the BIN directory. PE is not recommended for serious long term use as it does not have any of the features such as cut and paste which go to make these programs useful, however as it is supplied with full source code (as are all the utilities covered in this appendix) there is no reason why you should not add them once you become confident with the language. Indeed, because it can be modified in this way the only real limitation is the fact that as it is based on the memoedit() function it is unable to edit files greater than 64K in length (although as we have already seen, systems can be created using more than one source file so this limitation need not present too much of a problem).

When run, PE will ask for the name of the file to be edited and if an extension is not supplied a

.PRG file is assumed. If the file can not be found a new one is created, this file is then displayed for you to amend, however it is possible to pass the name of the file as a parameter to the program and hence prevent this question being asked. Most of the keys used by this editor are as you would expect those accepted by memoedit() (a full list of which can be found in chapter 3) however there are a few additions which are detailed below.

Alt-W	Save and continue
Alt-O	Change the filename
Alt-X	Exit
Alt-F	Display the filename
Alt-S	Search for a string
Alt-A	Search again
Alt-H	Display help

Report and label writer

The second utility that we shall look at in this appendix is the report and label writer. As the name suggests it is in fact two utilities rolled into one, the first being a report writer and the second a label writer, and although neither are very sophisticated they are sufficient for generating simple reports. When this utility is run by issuing the command RL from the MS-DOS command line you are presented with a menu containing the three options Report, Label, and Quit.

When report is selected you are prompted for the name of the report definition file you wish to edit. Having entered a filename you are then presented with the column definition screen in which you are prompted for information about each column. The first thing you are asked for is the contents of the column, this can be any expression (but to be of use this expression should be based on the file which will be open at the time the report is run). You will then be prompted for four lines of column header. This is followed by formatting information, the first being the column width, if the column is narrower than the information to be printed and the information is text then the text will be word wrapped onto subsequent lines, however if the information is numeric it will be replaced with asterisks. You are then prompted for the number of decimal places to be printed in the event that the column contains a numeric, this is followed by a logical indicating whether or not the numeric contents of the column should be totalled at the end of each group (or report if no groups are defined). Once columns have been defined it is possible to switch between them using the page up and page down keys, alternatively if you know the position number of the desired column it is possible to jump directly to it by pressing F7 and entering the number when prompted. If the contents field is empty the currently displayed column can be deleted by pressing F5 and if a new column is desired, then one can be inserted before the one currently being displayed by pressing F6. Pressing F2 takes you to the page definition screen in which you can enter the text to be used as a page header. Unlike the column headers which are printed even if they are blank, the page header is only used if text has been entered. This is followed by the page setup where you can define the size of the page and whether or not the text should be double spaced. After this you are able to state whether a form feed should be performed before and/or after the report and whether or not the header should be printed on subsequent pages. F3 allows you to define groups and sub-groups. Each group is defined by an expression and is given a title. It is also possible from this screen to suppress the individual lines of the report causing a brief summary (with any totals) to be produced, and if desired you can cause a form feed to be executed after each group has finished. The report definition can be exited at any time by pressing F10 whereupon if any changes have been made since the last time the definition was saved you will be prompted to save or abandon these changes. When the report has been defined it can be used by the REPORT FORM command (see chapter 3).

The label writer is far more simple but in many ways more useful. This writer contains only one screen. This screen is divided into two sections, which can be switched between using the F2 key. The top section contains the label definition including such things as the size of the labels and how many there are across the page, pressing F3 brings up a list of common label definitions from which you can choose, however you can define your own labels if they are of a different size. The bottom section allows you to state what should appear on the labels, the number of lines available in this section depends on the height entered in the top section. If the information required on a label is wider than the label the text will be truncated. Once saved (using the F10 key) this definition can be used by the LABEL FORM command (see chapter 3).

The database utility

The third utility supplied with CA-Clipper is DBU, this stands for the database utility and can be used to create data files along with their indexes. It can also be used to manipulate the data held in these files. When run, DBU can be passed any of three parameters (which, if used can be in any order), these are /c or /m to signify whether the display should be in colour or monochrome, /e signifying that files should be opened exclusive (for use on networks) and the name of the data or view file to be opened. If there is a data file and a view file with the same name the view file will be opened. The system consists of a series of menus across the top of the screen which can be activated at any time by pressing the associated function key, and a list of files across the rest of the screen over which the browse window is displayed when necessary. The file list consists of up to six columns in each of which the top file is the data file, beneath each is a list of up to seven indexes (with the top one being active), under these files is a list of the fields which will be browsed. DBU can only display a maximum of 64 fields, however using this list along with the insert and delete keys the order of these fields can be changed.

Note

Removing a field from the field list does just that, the file structure remains the same.

When a menu is selected, certain of its options may be unavailable due to whether a file is open and if so whether or not you are in browse (i.e. you can not pack a file if you haven't got one selected), in this event any options which are unavailable are 'greyed out'. Most of the menu options are self explanatory in that they refer to the CA-Clipper commands of the same name and any parameters needed are prompted for, the only ones which might cause confusion and are therefore covered here are those concerned with views. A view is all the data files which are open along with any indexes, filters, relationships and field lists. Once defined a view can be browsed using the view option from the browse menu (F5), however unlike browsing a data file you can not amend the contents of files while browsing them in this way. The one consideration to be made when opening files has to do with relationships, as relations can only be defined from left to right the parent file must be opened before the child. One of the omissions from CA-Clipper is that the view files created using this utility can not be used to open files in your own systems, however this can be overcome by calling the following function from your programs, it accepts the name of the view file and returns true if it is successful.

```
// opens the files and sets up the filters/relations
// held in the view file passed.

FUNCTION OpenView(cView)

    LOCAL nViewArea, cFile, nFile, nFileArea := {}
    LOCAL aFilter := {}, cFilter, cRelation, cAlias
    LOCAL aRelation := {}, nCounter, lRet := .t.

    cView += if(upper(right(alltrim(cView), 4)) != ;
      ".VEW", ".VEW", "")  // ensure the view filename
                           // includes the extension
    BEGIN SEQUENCE
        IF !file(cView)
            BREAK
        ENDIF

        dbusearea(.t., , cView)
        nViewArea := select()

        DO WHILE ! eof()
            // store any filters in the array aFilter
            DO WHILE left(alltrim(item_name), 2) == "kf"
                asize(aFilter, val(substr(item_name, 3, ;
                                                     1)))
                aFilter[len(aFilter)] := cContents()
            ENDDO
```

```
// open the .DBF files
DO WHILE alltrim(item_name) == "dbf"
    cFile := cContents()

    IF !file(cFile)
        break
    ENDIF

    dbusearea(.t., , cFile)
    aadd(nFileArea, select())
    select(nViewArea)
ENDDO

// open any indexes
DO WHILE left(item_name, 3) == "ntx"
    nFile := val(substr(item_name, 4, 1))
    cFile := cContents()
    select(nFileArea[nFile])

    IF !file(cFile)
        BREAK
    ENDIF

    dbsetindex(cFile)
    select(nViewArea)
ENDDO

// store the parent filenames of any
// relations to aRelation
DO WHILE alltrim(item_name) == "s_relate"
  aadd(aRelation, {substr(alltrim(contents),;
                  2), "", ""})
  SKIP
ENDDO

IF alltrim(item_name) == "k_relate"
// store the key expressions to aRelation
    FOR nCounter := 1 TO len(aRelation)
        aRelation[nCounter, 2] := ;
                    alltrim(contents)
        SKIP
    NEXT
ENDIF

IF alltrim(item_name) == "t_relate"
```

```
            // store the child filenames to aRelation
                FOR nCounter := 1 TO len(aRelation)
                    aRelation[nCounter, 3] := ;
                           substr(alltrim(contents), 2)
                    SKIP
                NEXT
            ENDIF
            SKIP
        ENDDO

        // set up any filters
        FOR nCounter := 1 TO len(aFilter)
            IF !empty(aFilter[nCounter])
                dbselectarea(nFileArea[nCounter])
                cFilter := aFilter[nCounter]
                SET FILTER TO &cFilter
            ENDIF
        NEXT

        // set up any relations
        FOR nCounter := 1 TO len(aRelation)
            dbselectarea(aRelation[nCounter, 1])
            cRelation := aRelation[nCounter, 2]
            cAlias    := aRelation[nCounter, 3]
            SET RELATION TO &cRelation INTO &cAlias;
                            additive
        NEXT

        select(nViewArea)
        CLOSE  // close the view file
    RECOVER
        lRet = .f.
    ENDSEQUENCE
RETURN lRet

// Returns the value held in the contents field.
// This value may span more than one record.

STATIC FUNCTION cContents

    LOCAL cString

    cString := contents
    SKIP
```

```
    DO WHILE empty(item_name)
        cString += contents
        SKIP
    ENDDO
RETURN cString
```

E Default file extensions

CH Header files used by the pre-processor have this extension.

CLD Script files used by the debugger have this extension.

DBF This extension denotes a database file.

DBT This extension is given to the file holding memo fields for the database file of the same name.

EXE Files with this extension can be executed by the computer.

FMT If a series of gets is defined for later use, it should be saved in a file with this extension.

FRM Report forms created by RL are given this extension.

INF RTLink saves the information it needs to perform incremental linking in files with this extension.

LBL Label definition files created using RL are saved with this extension.

LBR A library file used for holding related objects can be identified by this extension.

MAP This extension denotes a text file created by RTLink which contains the symbol and segment addresses used while linking.

NTX Any indexes created using the standard CA-Clipper indexing system are saved with this extension.

OBJ The output from the compiler is saved to a file with this extension.

OVL	Any external overlay files must have this extension.
PLL	A prelink library will have this extension (and must be available when the application is run).
PLT	Files with this extension are needed when a system requiring a prelinked library is linked .
PPO	The pre-processor output from the compiler can be saved using this extension.
PRG	Source files can be identified by this extension.
VEW	Database views used in DBU are saved with this extension.

F Example program

In this appendix we present a complete program to demonstrate how many of the features of the CA-Clipper language fit together. This program is a simple book cataloguing system which while not intended to be a definitive example of an application of this sort, does provide many good examples of how the functions and classes provided by CA-Clipper can be used. Throughout this program an attempt has been made to avoid the use of statements preferring their functional equivalents, however there are still some statements in CA-Clipper whose equivalent functions start with a double underscore indicating that they are internal functions and therefore should not be used by you as a programmer. We have also made use of the include file 'inkey.ch' which as has already been mentioned contains definitions for all the key codes returned by the inkey() function, this is in order that the code is more readable, a good example of which is the function lControl() which you first saw as the solution to problem 8.1 but which, with the use of this file is practically self documenting, another point to note is the fact that this program makes use of detached locals and codeblocks as parameters especially in the ListAuthor() and ListSubject() functions. The functions which make up this program are listed in alphabetical order with the exception of the function Books() which is the controlling function and therefore must be the first function in the file. If these functions are placed in a file called 'books.prg' it can be compiled using the /n switch.

```
#include "inkey.ch"
// This is the main routine of the system.
// It performs the menu handling.

FUNCTION Books

    LOCAL cColour, nOption := 1, cScreen, lLoop

    SET SCOREBOARD OFF
    lLoop   := .t.
    cColour := setcolor("w/b")
    cBox(0, 0, 24, 79, "╔═╗║╝═╚║ ")
    @ 1, 33 SAY "Book Catalogue."
    @ 2,  0 SAY "╠" + replicate("═", 78) + "╣"
    OpenFiles()

    DO WHILE lLoop
        cScreen := cBox(2, 32, 6, 48, "╔═╗║╝═╚║ ")
        @ 3, 33 PROMPT "Enter Data      "
        @ 4, 33 PROMPT "List by Author "
        @ 5, 33 PROMPT "List by Subject"
        MENU TO nOption
        restscreen(2, 32, 6, 48, cScreen)

        IF lastkey() == K_ESC
            lLoop := .f.
        ELSE
            DO CASE
                CASE nOption == 1
                    DataEntry()

                CASE nOption == 2
                    ListAuthor()

                CASE nOption == 3
                    ListSubject()
            ENDCASE
        ENDIF

    ENDDO

    setcolor(cColour)
    CLS
RETURN nil
```

```
// This routine handles the specific to the author lookup
// table.  It accepts the value of the key pressed, the
// tbrowse object and a reference to the author input
// variable.

FUNCTION AuthHandler(nKey, oBrowse, cAuthor)

    LOCAL cScreen, aAuthor := {"", ""}

    DO CASE
        CASE nKey == K_ENTER
            cAuthor := author->code

        CASE upper(chr(nKey)) == 'A'
            aAuthor[1] := "      "
            aAuthor[2] := space(30)

            IF lEditAuthor(aAuthor)
                dbappend()
                author->code   := aAuthor[1]
                author->author := aAuthor[2]
                oBrowse:refreshall()
            ENDIF

        CASE upper(chr(nKey)) == 'E' .and. !(eof();
                                           .and. bof())
            aAuthor[1] := author->code
            aAuthor[2] := author->author

            IF lEditAuthor(aAuthor)
                author->code   := aAuthor[1]
                author->author := aAuthor[2]
                oBrowse:refreshcurrent()
            ENDIF

    ENDCASE
RETURN nil

// This function performs the browse.  It accepts the
// tbrowse object and the handler to be called if the
// standard key handler can not action the key press.

FUNCTION Browse(oBrowse, bHandler)

    LOCAL nKey := 0
```

```
    DO WHILE nKey != K_ESC .and. nKey != K_ENTER
        stable(oBrowse)
        nKey := inkey(0)

        IF ! lControl(oBrowse, nKey)
            eval(bHandler, nKey, oBrowse)
        ENDIF

    ENDDO
RETURN nil

// Displays a box on the screen returning the original
// contents of the area. Accepts the coordinates of the
// box and the character string to be used.

FUNCTION cBox(nTop, nLeft, nBottom, nRight, cString)

    LOCAL cScreen

    cScreen := savescreen(nTop, nLeft, nBottom, nRight)
    dispbox(nTop, nLeft, nBottom, nRight, cString)
RETURN cScreen

// Accepts a string and returns the next string in
// alphabetical order by replacing the last character
// with the one with the next lowest ASCII value.

FUNCTION cNextCode(cCode)
RETURN left(cCode, len(cCode) - 1 ) + ;
                              chr(asc(right(cCode, 1)) + 1)

// Checks in AUTHOR.DBF that the author code entered is
// valid. If it is not performs a lookup box. Accepts the
// get object as input.

FUNCTION cValidAuthor(oGet)

    LOCAL cScreen, oAuthors, bAuthHandler, nTop := 4
    LOCAL nLeft := 38, cAuthor

    cAuthor := oGet:buffer

    IF !author->(dbseek(cAuthor))
        select("author")
        dbgotop()
```

```
      cScreen := cBox(nTop, nLeft, nTop + 13, nLeft + 38;
                                      , "╔╗║╝═╚║ ")
      @ nTop +  1, nLeft + 1 SAY "Code  Author"
      @ nTop +  2, nLeft SAY "╟" + replicate("─", 37) ;
                                                 + "╢"
      @ nTop + 11, nLeft SAY "╟" + replicate("─", 37) ;
                                                 + "╢"
      @ nTop + 12, nLeft + 2 SAY ;
               "A - Add.   E - Edit.   Cr - Select."

      oAuthors := tbrowsedb(nTop + 3, nLeft + 1, ;
                               nTop + 10, nLeft + 37)
      oAuthors:addcolumn(tbcolumnnew("", {||code}))
      oAuthors:addcolumn(tbcolumnnew("", {||author}))
      bAuthHandler := {|nKey, oBrowse| ;
                AuthHandler(nKey, oBrowse, @cAuthor)}

      Browse(oAuthors, bAuthHandler)
      restscreen(nTop, nLeft, nTop + 13, nLeft + 38 ;
                                          , cScreen)
      select("books")
      eval(oGet:block, cAuthor)

   ENDIF
RETURN .t.

// Checks in SUBJECT.DBF that the subject code entered is
// valid.  If it is not performs a lookup box. Accepts the
// get object as input.

FUNCTION cValidSubject(oGet)

   LOCAL cScreen, oSubjects, bSubHandler, nTop := 4
   LOCAL nLeft := 38, cSubject

   cSubject := oGet:buffer

   IF !subject->(dbseek(cSubject))
      select("subject")
      dbgotop()
      cScreen := cBox(nTop, nLeft, nTop + 13, ;
                              nLeft + 38, "╔╗║╝═╚║ ")
      @ nTop +  1, nLeft + 1 SAY "Code  Subject"
      @ nTop +  2, nLeft SAY "╟" + replicate("─", 37) ;
                                                + "╢"
```

```
        @ nTop + 11, nLeft SAY "╟" + replicate("─", 37) ;
                                                    + "╢"
        @ nTop + 12, nLeft + 2 SAY ;
                   "A - Add.   E - Edit.   Cr - Select."
        oSubjects := tbrowsedb(nTop + 3, nLeft + 1, nTop ;
                                   + 10, nLeft + 37)
        oSubjects:addcolumn(tbcolumnnew("", {||code}))
        oSubjects:addcolumn(tbcolumnnew("", {||subject}))
        bSubHandler := {|nKey, oBrowse| ;
                   SubHandler(nKey, oBrowse, @cSubject)}

        Browse(oSubjects, bSubHandler)
        restscreen(nTop, nLeft, nTop + 13, nLeft + 38, ;
                            cScreen)
        select("books")
        eval(oGet:block, cSubject)
    ENDIF
RETURN .t.

// Performs data entry for BOOKS.DBF. Validation is that
// the title must not be empty and that both the author and
// the subject codes must exist in their relevant files.
// Note the author and subject valid clauses are codeblocks
// to enable the get object to be passed to the valid
// functions. Data input will continue until escape is
// pressed.

FUNCTION DataEntry

    LOCAL nTop := 5, nLeft := 20, cTitle, cAuthor
    LOCAL cSubject, cScreen, GetList := {}, cPublished

    select("books")
    cScreen := cBox(nTop, nLeft, nTop + 4, nLeft + 47, ;
                                                "╓╖║╜═╙║ ")
    @ nTop, nLeft + 6 SAY "╤"
    @ nTop + 1, nLeft +  1 SAY "Title│"
    @ nTop + 2, nLeft SAY ;
       "╟────┴┬────┬─────────┬─────────┬───────┬────────╢"
    @ nTop + 3, nLeft +  1 SAY ;
       "Author│      │Published│         │Subject│"
    @ nTop + 4, nLeft +  7 SAY "╧"
    @ nTop + 4, nLeft + 13 SAY "╧"
    @ nTop + 4, nLeft + 23 SAY "╧"
    @ nTop + 4, nLeft + 32 SAY "╧"
```

```
    @ nTop + 4, nLeft + 40 SAY "±"

    DO WHILE lastkey() != K_ESC
        cTitle      := space(40)
        cAuthor     := "     "
        cPublished := ctod("  /  /  ")
        cSubject    := "     "
        lLoop       := .t.

        DO WHILE lLoop .and. lastkey() != K_ESC
            @ nTop + 1, nLeft +  7 GET cTitle    ;
                    PICTURE replicate("x", 40)  ;
                    VALID !empty(cTitle)
            @ nTop + 3, nLeft +  8 GET cAuthor  ;
                    PICTURE "xxxxx"             ;
                    VALID {|oGet|cValidAuthor(oGet)}
            @ nTop + 3, nLeft + 24 GET cPublished
            @ nTop + 3, nLeft + 41 GET cSubject ;
                    PICTURE "xxxxx"             ;
                    VALID {|oGet|cValidSubject(oGet)}
            READ

            lLoop := lSave(nTop + 3, nLeft + 30)

            IF !(lastkey() == K_ESC .or. lLoop)
                dbappend()
                books->title     := cTitle
                books->author    := cAuthor
                books->published := cPublished
                books->subject   := cSubject
            ENDIF

        ENDDO
    ENDDO
    restscreen(nTop, nLeft, nTop + 4, nLeft + 47, cScreen)
RETURN nil

// Performs default actions for each key press in the
// browse.  Accepts the tbrowse object and the value of the
// key pressed returning .t. if the key was actioned.

FUNCTION lControl(oBrowse, nKey)

    LOCAL lRet := .t.
```

```
DO CASE
    CASE nKey == K_HOME
        oBrowse:home()

    CASE nKey == K_CTRL_RIGHT
        oBrowse:panRight()

    CASE nKey == K_PGDN
        oBrowse:pageDown()

    CASE nKey == K_RIGHT
        oBrowse:right()

    CASE nKey == K_UP
        oBrowse:up()

    CASE nKey == K_END
        oBrowse:end()

    CASE nKey == K_PGUP
        oBrowse:pageUp()

    CASE nKey == K_LEFT
        oBrowse:left()

    CASE nKey == K_CTRL_END
        oBrowse:panEnd()

    CASE nKey == K_DOWN
        oBrowse:down()

    CASE nKey == K_CTRL_LEFT
        oBrowse:panLeft()

    CASE nKey == K_CTRL_HOME
        oBrowse:panHome()

    CASE nKey == K_CTRL_PGDN
        oBrowse:goBottom()

    CASE nKey == K_CTRL_PGUP
        oBrowse:goTop()

    OTHERWISE
        lRet := .f.
```

```
    ENDCASE
RETURN lRet


// New author input routine.  Will loop until the user
// selects 'save' or presses escape.  Accepts the reference
// of an array into which the input is stored and returns
// .t. if escape is pressed.

FUNCTION lEditAuthor(aAuthor)

    LOCAL cScreen, nTop := 10, nLeft := 18
    LOCAL GetList := {}, lLoop := .t.

    cScreen := cBox(nTop, nLeft, nTop + 4, nLeft + 36, ;
"╓╖║╜═╙║ ")
    @ nTop, nLeft + 5 SAY "╤"
    @ nTop + 1, nLeft + 1 SAY "Code│"
    @ nTop + 2, nLeft SAY "╟────┼" + replicate("─", 30) ;
                                              + "╢"
    @ nTop + 3, nLeft + 1 SAY "Name│"
    @ nTop + 4, nLeft + 5 SAY "╧"

    DO WHILE lLoop .and. lastkey() != K_ESC
        @ nTop + 1, nLeft + 6 GET aAuthor[1] ;
                              PICTURE "xxxxx"
        @ nTop + 3, nLeft + 6 GET aAuthor[2] ;
                              PICTURE replicate("x", 30)
        READ
        lLoop := lSave(nTop + 3, nLeft + 20)
    ENDDO

    restscreen(nTop, nLeft, nTop + 4, nLeft + 36, cScreen)
RETURN (lastkey() != K_ESC)


// New author input routine.  Will loop until the user
// selects 'save' or presses escape.  Accepts the reference
// of an array into which the input is stored and returns
// .t. if escape is pressed.

FUNCTION lEditSubject(aSubject)

    LOCAL cScreen, nTop := 10, nLeft := 18
    LOCAL GetList := {}, lLoop := .t.
```

```
    cScreen := cBox(nTop, nLeft, nTop + 4, nLeft + 36, ;
                                                "╓╖║╜═╙║ ")
    @ nTop, nLeft + 5 SAY "╤"
    @ nTop + 1, nLeft + 1 SAY "Code│"
    @ nTop + 2, nLeft SAY "╟────┼" + replicate("─", 30) ;
                                                      + "╢"
    @ nTop + 3, nLeft + 1 SAY "Name│"
    @ nTop + 4, nLeft + 5 SAY "╧"

    DO WHILE lLoop .and. lastkey() != K_ESC
        @ nTop + 1, nLeft + 6 GET aSubject[1] ;
                              PICTURE "xxxxx"
        @ nTop + 3, nLeft + 6 GET aSubject[2] ;
                              PICTURE replicate("x", 30)
        READ
        lLoop := lSave(nTop + 3, nLeft + 20)
    ENDDO

   restscreen(nTop, nLeft, nTop + 4, nLeft + 36, cScreen)
RETURN (lastkey() != K_ESC)


// Allows input of the author whose books are to be listed
// and then creates the browse.

FUNCTION ListAuthor

    LOCAL nTop := 7, nLeft := 30, cScreen, cAuthor
    LOCAL bFilter, oBrowse, GetList := {}
    select("books")
    dbsetorder(1)
    cAuthor := "     "
    cScreen := cBox(nTop, nLeft, nTop + 2, nLeft + 19, ;
                                                "╓╖║╜═╙║ ")
    @ nTop, nLeft + 13 SAY "╤"
    @ nTop + 1, nLeft +  1 SAY "Enter Author│"
    @ nTop + 2, nLeft + 13 SAY "╧"
    @ nTop + 1, nLeft + 14 GET cAuthor PICTURE "xxxxx" ;
                         VALID {|oGet|cValidAuthor(oGet)}
    read
    restscreen(nTop, nLeft, nTop + 2, nLeft + 19,        ;
                                                  cScreen)
    @ 4,  0 SAY "╟"
    @ 4, 79 SAY "╢"
    bFilter := {||books->author == cAuthor}
```

```
    dbsetrelation("author",  {||books->author})
    dbsetrelation("subject", {||books->subject})
    dbseek(cAuthor)
    oBrowse := tbrowsenew(3, 1, 23, 78)
    oBrowse:colsep  := "|"
    oBrowse:headsep := "—"
    oBrowse:addcolumn(tbcolumnnew("Title",           ;
                                               {||title}))
    oBrowse:addcolumn(tbcolumnnew("Author",          ;
                                        {||author->author}))
    oBrowse:addcolumn(tbcolumnnew("Published",       ;
                                            {||published}))
    oBrowse:addcolumn(tbcolumnnew("Subject",         ;
                                      {||subject->subject}))
    oBrowse:skipblock  := {|nRec|nSkipBlock(nRec, ;
                                                  bFilter)}
    oBrowse:gotopblock := {||dbseek(cAuthor)}
    oBrowse:gobottomblock :=                          ;
         {||dbseek(cNextCode(cAuthor), .t.), dbskip(-1)}
    Browse(oBrowse, {||.t.})
    @ 3,  1 clear to 23, 78
    @ 4,  0 SAY "║"
    @ 4, 79 SAY "║"
RETURN nil
```

// Allows input of the subject on which books are to be
// listed and then creates the browse.

```
FUNCTION ListSubject

   LOCAL nTop := 7, nLeft := 30, cScreen, cSubject
   LOCAL bFilter, oBrowse, GetList := {}
   select("books")
   dbsetorder(2)
   cSubject := "     "
   cScreen := cBox(nTop, nLeft, nTop + 2, nLeft + 20,  ;
                                           "╓╖║╜═╙║ ")
   @ nTop, nLeft + 14 SAY "╤"
   @ nTop + 1, nLeft +  1 SAY "Enter Subject|"
   @ nTop + 2, nLeft + 14 SAY "╧"
   @ nTop + 1, nLeft + 15 GET cSubject PICTURE "xxxxx" ;
                     VALID {|oGet|cValidSubject(oGet)}
   read
   restscreen(nTop, nLeft, nTop + 2, nLeft + 20,       ;
                                              cScreen)
```

```
  @ 4,  0 SAY "╟"
  @ 4, 79 SAY "╢"
   bFilter := {||books->subject == cSubject}
   dbsetrelation("author",  {||books->author})
   dbsetrelation("subject", {||books->subject})
   dbseek(cSubject)
   oBrowse := tbrowsenew(3, 1, 23, 78)
   oBrowse:colsep  := "│"
   oBrowse:headsep := "─"
   oBrowse:addcolumn(tbcolumnnew("Title",          ;
                                            {||title}))
   oBrowse:addcolumn(tbcolumnnew("Author",         ;
                                     {||author->author}))
   oBrowse:addcolumn(tbcolumnnew("Published",      ;
                                        {||published}))
   oBrowse:addcolumn(tbcolumnnew("Subject",        ;
                                   {||subject->subject}))
   oBrowse:skipblock  := {|nRec|nSkipBlock(nRec,  ;
                                             bFilter)}
   oBrowse:gotopblock := {||dbseek(cSubject)}
   oBrowse:gobottomblock :=                        ;
        {||dbseek(cNextCode(cSubject), .t.), dbskip(-1)}
   Browse(oBrowse, {||.t.})
   @ 3,  1 clear to 23, 78
   @ 4,  0 SAY "║"
   @ 4, 79 SAY "║"
RETURN nil


// An 'amend or save' menu which accepts the coordinates
// of the top left corner and returns .t. if amend is
// selected.

FUNCTION lSave(nTop, nLeft)

   LOCAL cScreen, nOption := 1

   IF lastkey() != K_ESC
     cScreen := cBox(nTop, nLeft, nTop + 3, nLeft + 6, ;
                                          "╔╗║╝═╚║ ")
     @ nTop + 1, nLeft + 1 PROMPT "Amend"
     @ nTop + 2, nLeft + 1 PROMPT "Save "
     MENU TO nOption
     restscreen(nTop, nLeft, nTop + 3, nLeft + 6,      ;
                                              cScreen)
```

```
    ENDIF
RETURN (nOption == 1)


// This is the skip block for the list of books by a
// specified author.  It accepts the number of records to
// be moved, and the authors code.  It uses this code to
// prevent the browse from moving outside the selected
// condition.  It returns the number of records moved.

FUNCTION nSkipBlock(nRec, bFilter)

    LOCAL nMoved := 0, nDirection

    IF nRec == 0
        dbskip(0)
    ELSE
        IF nRec > 0
            nDirection := 1
        ELSE
            nDirection := -1
        ENDIF

        DO WHILE nMoved != nRec .and. eval(bFilter) ;
                              .and. !eof() .and. !bof()
            dbskip(nDirection)
                nMoved += nDirection
            ENDDO

            DO CASE
                CASE eof() .and. nMoved != 0
                    dbskip(-1)
                    nMoved --

                CASE bof() .and. nMoved != 0
                    dbgoto(recno())
                    nMoved ++

                CASE !eval(bFilter) .and. nMoved != 0
                    dbskip(-nDirection)
                    nMoved -= nDirection
            ENDCASE
    ENDIF
RETURN nMoved
```

```
// This function opens the data files.  Before opening a
// file it checks for its existence and if not found the
// file is first created.

FUNCTION OpenFiles

    LOCAL aStruct

    IF file("books.dbf")
        dbusearea(.t.,,"books")
    ELSE
        aStruct := {}
        aadd(aStruct, {"title"     , 'C', 40, 0})
        aadd(aStruct, {"author"    , 'C',  5, 0})
        aadd(aStruct, {"published" , 'D',  8, 0})
        aadd(aStruct, {"subject"   , 'C',  5, 0})
        dbcreate("books", aStruct)
        dbusearea(.t.,,"books")
    ENDIF

    if ! file("books1.ntx")
       dbcreateindex("books1", "author", {||author}, .f.)
    endif

    if ! file("books2.ntx")
       dbcreateindex("books2", "subject", {||subject}, ;
                                                     .f.)
    endif

    dbclearindex()
    dbsetindex("books1")
    dbsetindex("books2")

    IF file("author.dbf")
        dbusearea(.t.,,"author")
    ELSE
        aStruct := {}
        aadd(aStruct, {"code",    'C',  5, 0})
        aadd(aStruct, {"author", 'C', 30, 0})
        dbcreate("author", aStruct)
        dbusearea(.t.,,"author")
    ENDIF

    IF file("author.ntx")
        dbsetindex("author")
```

```
    ELSE
        dbcreateindex("author", "code", {||code}, .f.)
    ENDIF

    IF file("subject.dbf")
        dbusearea(.t.,,"subject")
    ELSE
        aStruct := {}
        aadd(aStruct, {"code"    , 'C',  5, 0})
        aadd(aStruct, {"subject" , 'C', 30, 0})
        dbcreate("subject", aStruct)
        dbusearea(.t.,,"subject")
    ENDIF

    IF file("subject.ntx")
        dbsetindex("subject")
    ELSE
        dbcreateindex("subject", "code", {||code}, .f.)
    ENDIF
RETURN nil


// This function loops until the browse is stable, enabling
// the browse to be re-drawn without going back to the
// controlling loop. It accepts the tbrowse object.

FUNCTION stable(oBrowse)

    DO WHILE ! oBrowse:stabilize()
    ENDDO
RETURN nil


// This routine handles the specific to the subject lookup
// table.  It accepts the value of the key pressed, the
// tbrowse object and a reference to the subject input
// variable.

FUNCTION SubHandler(nKey, oBrowse, cSubject)

    LOCAL cScreen, aSubject := {"", ""}

    DO CASE
        CASE nKey == K_ENTER
            cSubject := subject->code
```

```
     CASE upper(chr(nKey)) == 'A'
          aSubject[1] := "     "
          aSubject[2] := space(30)

          IF lEditSubject(aSubject)
               dbappend()
               subject->code    := aSubject[1]
               subject->subject := aSubject[2]
               oBrowse:refreshall()
          ENDIF

     CASE upper(chr(nKey)) == 'E' .and. !(eof() .and. ;
                                                  bof())
          aSubject[1] := subject->code
          aSubject[2] := subject->subject

          IF lEditSubject(aSubject)
               subject->code   := aSubject[1]
               subject->author := aSubject[2]
               oBrowse:refreshcurrent()
          ENDIF
   ENDCASE
RETURN nil
```

Glossary

Class A combination of data structures and the functions used to manipulate those structures.

Compiler A language translator which converts a programs source code into a form which can be executed by a computer.

Constructor function
The function used to create an instance of an object is called its constructor function.

Context sensitive help
This is where the help provided is of direct relevance to the task which was being attempted at the time of the request. This means that help screens can be smaller, taking less time to read and thereby improving efficiency.

Data driven This is where the actions taken by the program are determined by parameters held in a file. In this way the same program can be made to behave in two different ways simply by passing it two different sets of parameters.

Double space
This is where a blank line is inserted between each line of information on a report.

Environment variables
These are MS-DOS variables which are defined using the set command and are used to modify the way

some programs work on your particular computer.

Event driven
This is when the flow of control through a program is defined by events which occur at run time (such as a key being pressed).

Get system The get system is the pre-defined class supplied with CA-Clipper to accept input from the user.

Greyed out To display an unavailable menu option in a different (usually lower intensity) colour.

Instance An instance of an object is an occurrence of it.

Instance variable
A variable which is held within an instance of an object is called an instance variable.

Interpreter An interpreter executes a programs source code directly without compiling it first. It does this by converting each line as it needs it.

Methods A function or routine which is stored within a class and performs actions upon that class is called a method.

Object A variable containing an instance of a class.

Overflow This is used to describe when a variable is displayed using a picture string which is too small. When this occurs a row of asterisks is displayed instead.

Pre-processor
A program which converts one state-

ment into one or more other statements. In CA-Clipper this occurs as the first stage of the compilation process.

Procedure driven
This is when the flow of control through the program is pre-defined by the programmer.

String variable
A string variable is a character variable which contains more than one character.

Shortcutting
The process of evaluating the smallest number of expressions to determine the outcome of a compound logical expression.

Wait state This is when the program is waiting for user input. It includes all input functions and commands other than inkey().

Word wrap This is the process of moving a word to the next line if there is insufficient space for it on the current line.

Index

& 4
&& 2
/* .. */ 2
// 2
? 28
?? 28
@ Clear 30
@ Get 35
@ Prompt 37
@ Say 32
@ To 30

A

Aadd 18
Achoice 80
Aclone 19
Acopy 19
AddColumn 86
Additive 73
Adel 18
Aeval 84
Afill 19
Ains 18
All 62, 69
Alltrim 16
And 52
Append 67
Append from 75
Array 5
Asc 48
Ascan 20
Asize 18
Asort 21
At 15
Atail 20

B

Background 39
Begin sequence 101
Blink 39
Block 5
Bof 72
Border 39
Break 101
Bright 39

C

Callstack 139
Case 54
Cdow 22
Character 4
Chr 48
Clear 29
Clipinit 51
Clippercmd 132
Close 62
Cls 30
Cmonth 22
Code 138
Col 29
Command 139
Comments 2
Continue 71
Copy to 74
Count 73
Ctod 22

D

DataBase Utility 146
Date 5, 22
Day 22
Dbclearindex 65
Dbcreate 60
Dbcreateindex 109
Dbeval 84
Dbseek 71
Dbselectarea 61
Dbsetindex 62
Dbusearea 62
Define 107
Delete 68
Deleted 68

Delimited 75
Descend 64
Detached locals 84
Devpos 29
Dispbox 31
Do 11
Dow 22
Dtoc 23
Dtos 23

E

Else 53
Empty 23
Endcase 55
Enddo 56
Endif 53
Enhanced 39
Eof 72
Errorblock 102
Errornew 103
Eval 83
Exit 50, 57

F

Fclose 78
Fcreate 76
Field 67
Fields 74
File 133
Filter 72, 88
Fopen 76
For 42, 56
Found 69
Fread 77
Fseek 77
Function 10
Fwrite 76

G

Get 6
Get/Set function 94
Getapplykey 98
Getlist 37
GetNew 95
Getreader 98
Go 69, 70
Gobottom 88
GoBottomBlock 87
Gotop 88
GoTopBlock 87

H

Help 91

I

If 53
In 68
Include 107
Index 63
Init 50
Inkey 48
Int 13
Isalpha 16
Iscolor 40
Isdigit 16
Islower 16
Isprinter 43
Isupper 16

L

Label definition file 43
Label form 43, 149
Lastkey 48
Left 14
Len 15, 20
Library 134
Local 3
Locate 71
Logical 5
Loop 57, 101
Lower 16
Ltrim 16

M

Macro 4, 111
Manifest constants 107
Max 14
Memo 5
Memoedit 43
Memoline 47

Memoread 46
Memowrit 46
Menu 37
Message 38
Mlcount 47
Monitor 139
Month 22

N

New 62
Next 56
Nextkey 48
Noconsole 42
Not 52
Note 2
Numeric 4

O

Objects 5
Operators 7
Or 52
Order 66
Otherwise 55
Output 134
Overlay 135

P

Pack 68
Parameter 11
Pcount 12
Picture 42
Pre-processor 106
Private 3
Procedure 9
Programmers editor 146
Pseudo-functions 107
Public 3

Q

Qout 28
Qqout 28

R

Rat 15
Read 37
Reader 98
Readmodal 97
Recall 68
Recno 72
Recover 101
Recover using 101
RefreshAll 89
RefreshCurrent 89
Reindex 68
Relation 73
Replace 67
Report and label writer 146
Report form 42, 149
Rest 72
Restscreen 32
Return 7, 101
Right 14
Row 29
Rtlinkcmd 134
Rtrim 16

S

Sample 43
Save 37
Savescreen 32
Say 6
SDF 74
Seek 69
Select 61
Set 111
Set Console 41
Set Device 41
Set Key 57
Set Printer 41
Set Printer To 75
Setcolor 39, 95
Skip 69
SkipBlock 87
Softseek 70
Stabilize 86
Standard 39
Static 4
Str 25
Substr 14
Sum 73
System Data Format 74

T

Tbcolumnnew 85
Tbrowse 85
Tbrowsedb 85
Tbrowsenew 85
Transform 42
Trim 16
Type 25

U

Unique 65
Unselected 39
Untransform 99
Upper 16
Use 62

V

Val 24
Valid 35
Valtype 25
Variables 3

W

Watch 139
When 35
While 42, 56
With 11, 75
Workareas 61

Y

Year 22

Z

Zap 68